The Best Cat Ever

Books by Cleveland Amory

NONFICTION

The Proper Bostonians
The Last Resorts
Who Killed Society?
Man Kind?
The Cat Who Came for Christmas
The Cat and the Curmudgeon
The Best Cat Ever

FICTION

Home Town
The Trouble with Nowadays

EDITOR

Celebrity Register
Vanity Fair Anthology

CLEVELAND AMORY

The Best Cat Ever

Illustrations by Lisa Adams

LITTLE, BROWN AND COMPANY

Boston   New York   Toronto   London

First Edition

Permissions to quote from copyrighted material
appear on page 262.

Library of Congress Cataloging-in-Publication Data
Amory, Cleveland.
    The best cat ever / Cleveland Amory; illustrations by Lisa Adams.
    — 1st ed.
        p.   cm.
    ISBN 0-316-03744-3
    1. Amory, Cleveland — Biography.   2. Authors, American — 20th
century — Biography.   3. Pet owners — United States — Biography.
4. Cats — United States — Anecdotes.   I. Title.
    PS3551.M58Z4614   1993
    818'.5403 — dc20
    [B]   93-28194

10   9   8   7   6   5   4   3   2

RRD-VA

*Published simultaneously in Canada
by Little, Brown & Company (Canada) Limited*

Printed in the United States of America

For Walter Anderson

Contents

The Best
Cat
Ever

Prologue

First, an apology. It is presumptuous of me to title this last book about the cat who owned me what I have titled it — *The Best Cat Ever*. The reason it is presumptuous is that to people who have, or have ever been, owned by a cat, the only cat who can ever be the best cat ever is their cat.

I understand this, but still I beg your indulgence. Please remember I am writing this only a short time after Polar Bear has gone, and writing about him is not now an easy task.

I guess it is never easy to write about a cat when he or she has gone. Of course, it is not so easy to write about them when they are around, either. Cats have difficulty standing still for portraits, whether in pictures or in a memoir, and they do so many different things and do them so quickly and change so fast that I really believe what we all should do when they are still around is to keep a diary.

Unfortunately, few of us do this, and although I have already written two other books about Polar Bear, I realize I missed much. But not, of course, anything like how much I miss him. I had already learned that writing about him was a much more difficult task than matters like either quickness of movement or of change. But I still had something else to learn — the awful truth that now when I write about the funniest things he ever did I do not want to laugh, I want to cry.

Nonetheless, I shall not inflict that, or anyway as little as possible of that, upon you. Polar Bear, who, just by being himself, did so much for so many stray cats — in twenty countries — deserves better. And I promise you, I shall do my best to see that he gets it.

I shall try, in other words, not to dwell on the present and the awful missing of him. I shall dwell, rather, on the past and the fun we had for the fifteen years we had together.

If I succeed in doing this I know you will pardon me for calling this book what I have called it, because one of the things I used to call him, in our special moments together, was the best cat ever.

In this book you will read that there is a small monument to Polar Bear at the Fund for Animals' Black Beauty Ranch in Murchison, Texas. The inscription on that monument states that that is where he is buried. Although I wrote that inscription, I do not want you to believe it. Where he is really buried, and where he is, and where he will always be, is in my heart.

CHAPTER ONE

A Cat for All Seasons

It has long been a theory of mine — and I am known, if I do say so, for my long theories — that authors, generally speaking, are rotten letter writers. There are good reasons for this. The good letter writer is writing privately, thinking of one person and writing intimately to that person. The author, on the other hand, who is not particularly accustomed to writing privately but rather to writing publicly, is not thinking of any one particular person except perhaps — and sometimes all too often — himself or herself.

And, speaking of that him and her, it is another theory

of mine that women, generally speaking, are better letter writers than men. There is a wide variety of good reasons for this, but the one which I believe has most merit is that women are superior in one-on-onemanship, if they will kindly forgive the male intrusion in that last word.

If authors are not that terrific at letter writing, however, they do appreciate good letter writing when they receive it. Indeed, one of the greatest pleasures authors have is reading letters addressed to them about what they write. I am no exception, and since my most recent books have concerned, among other things, my cat Polar Bear, I am particularly pleased about the number of people who write to me wanting to know more about him. Once in a while of course I wish that at least a few of these writers would also want to know more about me but, as I have often said, you can't have everything — particularly nowadays. You would think, though, that a reasonable number of people would take the time to figure out who did all the behind-the-scenes work, all of the dirty work in the trenches if you will, which made Polar Bear possible. But no, they don't. It's the star they want, and never mind the man without whom Polar Bear would never have been heard of, let alone been a star.

I was not the least jealous of Polar Bear, mind you, but I do want you to know that if the situation were reversed and more people wanted to know about me than about him he would not for a moment have been as philosophical about it as I was. As a matter of fact, I can see him now going right into one of his snits — and I tell you when it came to being jealous Polar Bear could go into the snottiest little snit you ever saw. Kindly remember that jealousy has often been described as "The Green-Eyed

Monster," and after you've done that just stop and ask yourself what color eyes do you think Polar Bear had?

There is, though, one question an extraordinary number of these letter writers asked which I found irritating for an entirely different reason from the ones who ignored me, and that was, very simply, the question they asked as to whether or not Polar Bear was still alive. I found these letters particularly annoying when he was still alive, and they are of course much more difficult to answer now. After all, I don't go around asking whether or not someone I know whom I also know that they know is dead yet. Just the same, that is the way "still alive" always sounded to me. In fact, still alive still sounds to me a dead ringer for dead yet.

Letter writers who were, to my mind, more considerate of my feelings were inclined to ask simply how old Polar Bear was. I liked that better, but I do believe that at a certain age, whether it is about cats or people, the question of how old one is has a certain annoyance to it. You do not meet someone you have not seen for some time and suddenly ask how old he or she is. It implies that they are not as young as they were. My answer to that is, who is?

The best answer to this question was given many years ago by a famous friend of mine — and also Polar Bear's — the late Cary Grant. Faced with a wire from a researcher from *Time* magazine which asked, "HOW OLD CARY GRANT?" Cary himself politely wired back. "OLD CARY GRANT FINE," he said. "HOW YOU?"

In any case, to answer my letter writers, I always made clear, at least until now, when he is gone, that Polar Bear was indeed alive and well. I rescued him, as I made very clear in *The Cat Who Came for Christmas*, on Christmas Eve,

1978, which made him in 1992, fourteen years older than he was when I rescued him.

There remains, of course, the sticky question as to how old he was in 1992. He was at least fourteen years more than when I rescued him, but how much more? In other words, how old was he when I rescued him? Remember, he was a stray, and strays do not come with birth certificates. Susan Thompson, his veterinarian, believes he could have been any age between one and three, but she is the first to admit that veterinarians have a very difficult time estimating cats' ages exactly. Horses, yes, apparently by their teeth, but cats no. Cats have very odd teeth anyway.

Marian Probst, my longtime assistant, believes Polar Bear was less than one, but I don't want you to go to the bank on Marian's opinion about his age, either. For example, Marian is always adding a year to my age for no reason at all, although I've told her a hundred times that because I was born in 1917 and it is now 1992 that does not make me seventy-five, it makes me seventy-four. After all I was *born* in 1917 — I wasn't *one* in 1917 — I was *zero* in 1917, and I wasn't anywhere near one until 1918. But it is no use talking figures with Marian — you might as well talk the economy.

Anyway, going along with Susan's doubt and ignoring Marian's mathematics, it is quite possible to assume that Polar Bear, who could well have been zero in 1978 was, let us say, zero until 1979. By the same figuring, I was sixty-one in 1979 — in the prime of life, if I do say so. Today I am a little past my prime, perhaps, but not much, mind you, just on the rim of my prime. On the other hand, in 1992, Polar Bear was, as I say, at least fourteen. Now,

I realize that when it comes to comparing cats' ages to people's ages an extraordinary number of people still believe that old wives' nonsense that seven years of your life is like one year of your cat's life. By that standard Polar Bear was, by a person's age, ninety-eight. How many people do you know who, at ninety-eight, are still alive? I know there are some, but I am asking how many.

And besides this I have literally hundreds of letters from people whose cats are in their twenties, and an extraordinary number whose cats are over twenty-five. That would make them, for a person, 175. The next time you see a person who is 175 please let me know, and while you're at it you might as well also tell him or her that, despite what Marian says, he or she is only 174.

I am, of course, not the only person who has called attention to the fallacy of that 7-to-1 cat-versus-person theory. Not long ago a veterinarian in the Gaines Research Center came up with a new chart — one which I have already published in a previous book but which I am now publishing again, for the benefit of those of you, and there are so many nowadays, who have poor memories. In any case, here it is:

Cat's Age	Person's Age
6 months	10 years
8 months	13 years
12 months	15 years
2 years	24 years
4 years	32 years
6 years	40 years

8 years	48 years
10 years	56 years
12 years	64 years
14 years	72 years
16 years	80 years
18 years	88 years
20 years	96 years
21 years	100 years

To my way of thinking this is certainly a lot closer to the mark than that old 7-to-1 theory, and it is rather remarkable how Gaines refuted that 7-to-1 by having the person go three years while the cat was going only from six months to eight months, and yet having the person at the advanced age of ninety-six go just four years to one hundred while the cat went only one year, from twenty to twenty-one. In any case, Gaines was not by any means alone in changing the 7-to-1 formula. In a British cat book, for example, I found the statement that some experts believe once a cat is nearing "feline old age" you should "multiply its years by 10 to get a true comparison with a person's age." And a British-born veterinarian now living in this country, Ian Dunbar, came up with a shorter revision:

Cat's Age	Person's Age
1 year	3 years
7 years	21 years
14 years	45 years
21 years	70 years
28 years	95 years
31 years	103 years

Shortly after the publication of his findings, Dr. Dunbar was challenged by Washington writer Ed Kane, who took him to task in three specific areas — of his cats' one to humans' three, of his cats' seven to humans' twenty-one, and of his cats' fourteen to humans' forty-five. Mr. Kane also recommended a study of cat-versus-human age by Dr. Tom Reichenbach. This, I learned, first appeared in *Feline Practice*, a veterinary journal, and in it Dr. Reichenbach went so far as to use a computer to compare the ages of some 480 cats and the data obtained from census records on human ages. He also completed a graph which demonstrated the comparison of one- to-seventeen-year-old cats with zero- to ninety-year-old humans. You may be sure I was very happy to see that zero recognized. In any case Dr. Reichenbach came up with these findings:

Cat's Age	Person's Age
1 year	17 years
2 years	28 years
3 years	31 years
4 years	41 years
5 years	45 years
6 years	45 years
7 years	51 years
8 years	58 years
9 years	61 years
10 years	61 years
11 years	66 years
12 years	66 years
13 years	71 years

14 years	76 years
15 years	81 years
16 years	81 years
17 years	89 years

I found some of these figures fascinating. For example, in the year when the cat went from five to six, the person stayed at forty-five, and in the year when the cat went from nine to ten, the person stayed at sixty-one. And still again, when the cat went from eleven to twelve, the person stayed at sixty-six. Finally, when the cat went from fifteen to sixteen, the person stayed at eighty-one. It was especially good to know that when Polar Bear was going from five to six and nine to ten and eleven to twelve, I was staying absolutely still. Who says everybody has to keep growing older? You don't, if you put your mind to it.

One thing was certain. If Polar Bear at fourteen was like me at seventy-four — I know the damned graph said seventy-six, but it could well have been a mistake — we were in a sense roughly the same age. At least we were both by no means old, but in the full bloom of what I would call our maturity. At the same time I realized I would now have to watch out for him more carefully. In just one more year, at fifteen, he would be like me in my eighties. Fifteen might not seem too bad for him to think about, but certainly the eighties were something I did not want to dwell on. What I did want to do was go back to some of the letters I had received from people who had cats over thirty. Dr. Dunbar had given a cat's age at thirty-one as a person's age at one hundred three. I was not really looking forward to being one hundred three, but from where I was sitting it was certainly a lot more appealing than Reichenbach's having Polar Bear being fourteen and me being just four years away from those damned eighties.

No matter. Whatever the age relationship between us, and whether or not I was in the prime, or on the rim, of my maturity, it was time for me to realize that, whatever I was, Polar Bear was no spring chicken. And so, whether he liked it or not, I had better get on with an entirely new health and fitness program for him. The first thing I did was to read everything I could get my hands on pertaining to older cats. One of the first was a book by Harry Miller entitled *The Common Sense Book of Kitten and Cat Care.* "Cats generally begin to show their age," he wrote, "at about 8 years." Frankly, that made me pretty mad. Polar Bear had not done anything of the sort at age eight and in fact at fourteen he still had not. But Mr. Miller went on:

> The elderly cat does not jump and run in play as he used to do. He is no longer capable of sustained exertion, and he may even tire after moderate exercise. He'll want to sleep more, and may be short-tempered about things he once put up with.

Again, that was not Polar Bear. He jumped and ran and played just the way he always did. He certainly did not tire after moderate exercise. It is true he wanted to sleep more, but I have never known him when he did not want to sleep more. Finally, as far as being short-tempered about things he once put up with, he never did put up with things he once put up with, for the simple reason that he never put up with them in the first place.

Frankly that opinion came too close to home for comfort. Finally, there was perhaps the most extraordinary opinion from my old friend Dr. Dunbar. He wrote in *Cat Fancy* magazine about a California cat named "Mother Cat" who, he said, had two hundred kittens and nonetheless lived to be thirty-one. She also, he maintained, liked both other cats and people, but she liked people more and more as she grew older. I could certainly understand that. At least I am sure by that time she liked people better than male cats. Dr. Dunbar, however, proceeded:

> As with Mother Cat, some cats like people more and more as they grow older. Other cats like people less and less, becoming increasingly intolerant of being disturbed and handled, especially by children and strangers.

Since Polar Bear was intolerant of children and strangers by the time I first saw him, he was, by fourteen, totally so. Nonetheless, Dr. Dunbar then went on with a suggestion about how to handle older cats when it came to what he called "even routine visits to the veterinarian."

> Do not wait for your middle-aged cat to become old and grouchy. Do something about it now. Prevention is the name of the game.

Dr. Dunbar was not kidding — and a game was indeed what he had in mind, as we shall see in a moment. First, though, he begins with how to prepare your cat for the experience:

> To prepare the cat to enjoy veterinary examinations, begin by introducing your cat to visitors. A simple and

ultimately enjoyable exercise is to invite people over to the house to hand-feed the cat its dinner. Refusal to take food from a stranger is a sign that the cat is stressed. Your job is to remove this stress before your cat's next routine veterinary examination. Do not rush, however; let the cat do things in its own good time. Forget the cat's dinner for today, and have the stranger try again tomorrow. Remember, it is quite normal for wild *Felidae* to go several days with no food at all. With patience and perseverance, any cat will come around eventually.

With all due respect to Dr. Dunbar, I could visualize all too clearly what would happen if I were to try the very idea of giving Polar Bear his dinner by hands-on feeding from strangers. Even if they were relatively familiar strangers, I assure you, they very soon would have a lot more to worry about than whether or not wild *Felidae* had or had not eaten for days — such as, for example, whether or not they still had the use of their own extremities to eat with.

But Dr. Dunbar apparently had not had that much experience with cats who felt as strongly about strangers as Polar Bear. Because, after the hands-on feeding, he proceeded right on to his promised games:

When the cat enjoys the company of strangers, it is party time — time to play Pass the Cat. One visitor picks up the cat, offers a treat, performs a cursory examination, offers a second treat, and then passes the cat to the next person. This game puts the cat in good stead for a visit to the veterinary clinic, especially if one or two visitors dress up as ersatz veterinarians — wearing white coats or surgery greens and sporting an antiseptic after-shave.

This one was, frankly, too much for me even to attempt to visualize. I just knew that when stranger A passed Polar Bear to stranger B, let alone on to strangers C, D, and E, that would be it because the stranger never lived who could handle a passed Polar Bear, game or no game. As for the game preparing Polar Bear for meeting a white- or green-coated "ersatz veterinarian" sporting "an antiseptic after-shave" I think one visit from Polar Bear would, at the very least, persuade a stranger to part company with the white or green coat and the antiseptic after-shave as rapidly as possible. And my advice to said stranger would be, after carefully shutting the door behind him before the advance of Polar Bear, to enter, again as rapidly as possible, some other ersatz field of endeavor.

I do not wish to give the impression that Polar Bear was, in his latter years, more difficult than he was when he was younger. Actually, that would not be fair — in many ways he was less difficult. When, for example, two strangers came to my apartment, he would often not bother to move from the chair in which he was sleeping. When he was younger, one stranger was his limit. Two, and in a flash he was off under the bed or under the sofa, and woe betide the stranger who tried to "Here Kitty Kitty" him from under there. Polar Bear was better when he was older, I believe, partly because it was more trouble for him to move. But equally partly I believe it was because as he grew older he grew more philosophical.

In 1991 *Cat Fancy* magazine did a survey of older cats — approximately one-third of whom were from ages ten to twelve, another third from thirteen to fifteen, and still another third from sixteen to nineteen. An extraordinary number of even the oldest of these cats were still lively and, just as I found with Polar Bear, at least a little friendlier with strangers. I liked best the comment of Andrea Dorn of Nevada, Ohio: "I'm not sure whether my cat's personality has changed or not," Andrea said. "I'll think she has become friendlier, but then she'll meet a new person and make a bad impression, and I realize that she and I just get along better. She hasn't really changed; I've just become more like her."

The more I thought about that story the more I thought that through the years Polar Bear and I had gotten more and more like each other. But I do think I should say that, while I had made a real effort to emulate his good qualities and not his bad ones, I do not feel he made the same effort in that department toward me. All too often I found him not emulating my good qualities, but emulating my very worst qualities. For example, I found him growing increasingly short of patience. I know patience is not my long suit, but I saw no reason for him to emulate that minor fault of mine when he could have much more profitably been working on one of my many major virtues, such as my unfailing courtesy to my inferiors. Which, if I do say so, keeps me very busy indeed.

But no matter. The point is that, generally speaking, we got along famously and, as I have said, knowing Polar Bear was, as the age comparisons showed, aging far more rapidly than I was, I made allowances for his character failings just the way I kept a careful check on his health and fitness. I had particular trouble with his eating. After years when he was younger of trying to keep him from getting too fat, now when he was older I was suddenly faced with the problem of him getting too thin. In the early days he was fussy about food, all right, but only fussy when I tried to put him on a diet. In later days, however, he was just fussy, period. It made no difference what I put down. He would sniff it and look at me, and all but say "You don't expect me to eat this, do you?" So, naturally, I would try something else. I usually had the same response again, and indeed it often took a third choice for him to get interested. Too often his average meal took on the appearance of a smorgasbord.

I was relieved to learn it was not at all unusual for older cats to eat less and to lose weight. But it worried me, and I fussed and fussed over it. I called his vet, Susan Thompson, on the slightest provocation, and when I claimed, as I usually did, that he was too sick to travel to the vet's, she graciously made a house call. She kept reassuring me that he was doing fine, but she also told me the fact was sooner or later I should know he would get sick.

I hated her telling me that. I hated it when Polar Bear was sick when he was younger, but when he was older, and he was in the twilight of his years, I did not think I could stand it. Just the same, I knew it was inevitable, and I tried to be a good soldier and brace myself for it. I also did my best to do everything I could for him.

And then like a bolt out of the blue came the shock — the very last thing I would expect. Polar Bear did not get sick — I got sick.

It was really incredible. Me, in the prime or on the rim, as I said, of my maturity, being the one to succumb, while Polar Bear, despite being the one far more precarious on the cat-age versus human-age scale and the one of the two of us who, by any odds, should have politely led the way toward any infirmity, was fine and dandy. Honestly, it was so unbelievable I could hardly make any sense out of it, let alone start to live with it.

As I have tried to make clear from the first book about Polar Bear, he and I were from the beginning two very different individuals when we were sick. When I was sick I wanted attention. I wanted it now, and I wanted it around the clock. Besides this, I wished everyone within earshot of my moans and groans, of which I have a wide variety, to know that I am not only at Death's door but also that I have the very worst case of whatever it is I think I have that has ever been visited on any man, woman, child or beast since the world began.

I stated clearly that if, for example, I had a slight cold and the cold had taken a turn for the worse, I wished people to gather around my bedside in respectful silence. For those with poor hearing, I wished them to gather especially close, and for those with poor memories I wished them to bring pad and pencil so that of course they could take down and transmit to posterity, hoarsely and with extreme difficulty, my last words. In much the same manner I visualized my loved ones gathering around after I had gone to my Final Reward to hear my Last Will and Testament. In this I fully intended to give them further instruction, since they no longer had the benefit of my counsel, on how they were to conduct themselves.

All this, mind you, for a cold. But now I had something far more severe — a combination of an ulcer, a distorted aneurism, and what my doctor, Anthony Grieco, described, after a look at my X-rays, as a "curmudgeonly esophagus." I know I have often been described as a curmudgeon, but to hear one's esophagus described in this way — and by one's own doctor — was a bit unsettling. Furthermore, since I was struck with all these troubles at once, I did not even have the time or opportunity to settle down into my usual hypochondriacal ways heretofore described. Instead I was just another patient — and one who, unhappily, as I believe I have already mentioned, was born without any patience.

The most curious thing of all is what happened to my relationship with Polar Bear. Instead of my looking after him, he was now looking after me. No longer was he the rescuee, as had happened in the beginning when I had found him that snowy Christmas Eve, when I found him outside the garage, now he was the rescuer. It really was a total turnaround from what had been our relationship since that first day.

Of course, he was not the only one looking after me. And Polar Bear was never good at being one of a group doing something together as a team. He was either the captain, or he would not play. In this case, if he could not be chief cook and bottle washer, he wanted to be chief of everything else. During the daytime he would sit at the far corner of the bed nearest the door and monitor all comings and goings with the authority of Horatius at the Bridge. During the nighttime he would hunker down between my arm and chest, making sure the covers allowed him to keep at least one beady eye ready for examining any nocturnal visitor.

If the person entering was Marian, my daughter, a friend, or even a long-standing enemy whom I had returned to grace, Polar Bear would of course motion them through, acting for all the world like a traffic patrolman. On the other hand, if the person were a stranger, out would come not only the paw to stop traffic, but the rest of Polar Bear, too. He did not actually attack people, but he certainly gave every indication of not being above such measures if required.

Watching him, I could not help thinking of a story I had read of another protective cat. The cat's name was Inkee, and he was owned by a woman named Debra Lewis of Detroit. One day, Mrs. Lewis remembered, she and her husband were playing on the floor. Inkee was in another room. Suddenly Mrs. Lewis yelled, "Ouch!" Immediately Inkee arrived on the double. His actions were, she reported, in order, first to sit on Mrs. Lewis' chest as if to say "Are you all right?" second, when Mrs. Lewis assured him she was, to kiss her on the nose; third, to go over to her husband and bite him; and fourth and finally, to run out of the room.

I sincerely believe that, faced with similar circumstances and substituting Mrs. Lewis for myself, Polar Bear would have done all of the above. I am particularly sure he would have done so in the case of the most difficult person with whom he had to cope during my illness — the trained nurse. Polar Bear did not like nurses, trained or not, and nurses did not like Polar Bear. For one thing he is not fond of people in white — on the theory, I believe, that their people-caring is just a front and that, underneath, they are probably veterinarians preparing at any time for a surreptitious assault with a needle.

There was another reason that Polar Bear did not like this particular nurse, and that was that he did not like her voice. Whether it was what she said with that voice or whether it was the way she said it — her maddening use of the plural, the endless "How are we?" addressed, of course, to just me — I do not know. But it was certainly one of the reasons he did not like her. There was, finally, a third reason he could not stand the nurse, and that was that I did not like her either, and he was smart enough to know that, and also to know that the reason I did not like her was primarily that she did not like him.

Fortunately this round robin did not last long. Her stay, however, brief as it was, had a bearing on Polar Bear's crowning achievement as watch-and-guard cat. This was the day, or rather the night, he spent with me in the hospital. I shall not tell you which hospital it was. Actually, I was in two of them — in Texas, where the attack first came on, and also in New York. But to spare the attendants of both of them — none of whom, I wish to point out, I actually physically abused — I shall not mention the hospitals' names.

There was a reason Polar Bear was at the hospital. Marian, who could not visit me that day, had a friend bring Polar Bear down in his carrier to see me. The friend was supposed to return before visiting hours were over and take Polar Bear back, but unfortunately an emergency came up and she could not make it. Since that particular day and night the other bed in the two-bed room was unoccupied, I decided that if Polar Bear spent the night he would at least not be bothering anybody else. I even took the precaution of spreading some newspaper in the bathroom for a serviceable litterbox.

If I had asked Marian to leave Polar Bear with me for the night, I very much doubt she would have done so. Marian plays strictly by the book — not, I am sorry to say, always by one of my books — and when it comes to rules and regulations I am firmly convinced that she, not Robert, wrote those rules of order. All in all, I was fortunate that night to have the friend bring Polar Bear and then not be able to return, although I must admit that when it happened I immediately began practicing my favorite winning argument in any situation — that "they" said it would be all right. Those "theys" may have been entirely fictitious, but I promise you they have covered a multitude of sins in my life, and in this case they came through with flying colors.

I did, however, have a serious talk with Polar Bear. I told him that during the night an almost steady stream of people would be passing through our room because that is the way hospitals work — they were sort of like railroad stations. Furthermore, I warned him, most of the people who would be passing in or through the room would be dressed in white, but he would not in any circumstance regard them as veterinarians. Indeed, I told him, he was not to regard them at all because I wished him, from the moment he heard footsteps approaching outside the door, to get under the covers and stay there without leaving in view even so much as one of his beady eyes.

I could tell by his tone of listening — and do not fool yourself, Polar Bear did indeed have a tone of listening — that he did not go along with my idea about this. Clearly, he wanted to know that if this was how it was going to be in the hospital, how in the world could I expect him to do his job of protecting me?

There are all kinds of protection, I told him sternly, just the way there are those who also serve who only stand and wait. They also protect, I added to make it absolutely clear, who only lie and wait. But lie and wait, I added firmly, was just what I expected him to do.

.

I next told him our first trouble would be the arrival of my supper. The minute I said "supper," Polar Bear could not see what trouble that could possibly be. I explained that it would be trouble because it would probably be brought by a man or a woman in white, and before he started to jump out of bed and up on the tray it would be nice if he at least waited until the man or woman had put the tray down.

I was of course being sarcastic. I didn't want under any condition for him to appear until the man or woman in white had left not only the tray, but also the room.

Polar Bear had the clearest way of asking, "And where, may I ask, do I come in?" The way he did it was by coming as close as a cat can to a cocked eyebrow. I told him he came in because the minute the man or woman went, then and only then could he come out and share my supper. And amazingly enough, it all happened exactly as we discussed it. The minute I heard the wheels of the meal cart outside the door I swooped Polar Bear under the covers and the man came in, put down the tray, and left, all so quickly that Polar Bear did not have time to do anything about it. Once we were alone, however, out he came, and dove for the supper tray. And so, between us, as we so often did at home, we shared and shared alike, his idea of sharing and sharing alike being that he ate both his share and my share of what he liked and left me to have both my share and his share of what he did not like.

When we were through I again placed him under the covers until the man had come in and removed the tray. Afterwards, I warned Polar Bear that we were far from out of the woods yet. Still to come, I told him, were at least three more visits. I also told him that, from then on, one or the other of us should stay awake and that we should schedule watches the way they do on shipboard. Since by this time Polar Bear was already yawning his head off — which was a tendency he often had when I was starting on something important — I decided to teach him a lesson and told him I would take the first shift from ten to twelve, and he could then take what I explained to him was the beginning of the graveyard shift, from twelve to two, and then again I would take over from two to four. There were only two troubles with this beautifully thought-out plan of mine. For one thing, we did not have an alarm clock, and for another we did not know exactly what our battle plan would be when the one who was on watch called the other to action. Actually, Polar Bear was terrific at waking me when he wanted something, but I had no idea how good he would be at waking me when he did not want something or wanted something to stop.

Anyway, we were in the middle of all these plans when suddenly I heard footsteps and the door opened and we had our first visitor. She turned on the light, moved swiftly to my bed, and put down a tray with some water and a pill in a cup. "It's our medication," she said. So far she had not even looked at me or the bed and I was sure she had not seen Polar Bear. But now she was turning and would see Polar Bear. Polar Bear, however, was nowhere to be seen. He was back under the covers. What he had done of course was to see the pill — and all I can say is that if I have ever seen a cat show the white feather I saw it then. I knew perfectly well how Polar Bear felt about pills, but this was too much. When it was all over and he came out, I had to explain to him what showing a white feather meant. I told him that it was plain and simple cowardice. He wanted to know where it came from, and I told him never mind where it came from, he would not remember it anyway. Actually, I learned it came from the belief that a gamecock with a white feather in his tail would not be a good fighter, and I did not see any reason for bringing up such a sordid subject as cockfighting.

I really gave him a very good speech, but the last part of it fell upon deaf ears. He had fallen asleep again. This of course I could not permit. It was now his watch, and people who went to sleep on their watch were often shot. Also I told him I particularly did not want him to go to sleep again before the sleeping pill nurse came — because sleeping pill nurses get very angry when patients go to sleep on them before they have had a chance to give them their pills. I informed Polar Bear sternly I simply would not answer for the consequences if the sleeping pill nurse saw him under such circumstances — it would be bad enough if she saw him under normal circumstances.

Once more I dozed off, and once more it seemed only a short time before the door opened again and this time the lights came flooding on as well as the cheerful question, "How are we tonight?" All I could do was reply wanly that I was as well as could be expected. Once more there was, of course, no Polar Bear in evidence. He was under the covers again, sleeping on picket duty — really he was impossible — particularly since we were this time faced with the temperature-and-pulse nurse. First she put the thermometer in my mouth and then reached for my wrist. This was a mistake. Polar Bear almost invariably took exception to strangers attempting intimacies with me. Out came, all too visibly, one of his arms with its paw headed ominously for the nurse's hand. I had a brief thought that what we would now have would be a three-person arm wrestle, but unfortunately the situation was far worse than I thought. The nurse could not fail to see Polar Bear's arm appear from under the covers, but that was not the main trouble. The main trouble was that she did not think the arm belonged to a cat. What she thought it belonged to was far worse — she thought it belonged to a snake. In any case she shrieked her displeasure, jumped up and made a mess of everything, including the thermometer in my mouth.

At this juncture I could hear steps coming down the hall — probably, I thought, the nurses' guard. Immediately I took the thermometer out of my mouth and reached under the covers where, good as gold, Polar Bear still was. I pulled him out and held him up, in all his glory, for the nurse to see. See, I said, no snake, no snake at all, just a dear little cat.

By this time she did not know what to think, but it was Polar Bear who saved the day. He did not hiss at her or do anything threatening, but instead gave a definite purr and then one of his perfected silent AEIOU's. It won her over in an instant — in fact, before her nurses' guard appeared, she had actually helped me to get Polar Bear back under the covers. By the time they marched in I was having both my temperature and pulse taken as if nothing had happened.

Our third visitor was the sleeping pill nurse, and from the beginning we were off to a bad start. Despite what I had explicitly told Polar Bear not to do, he was sound asleep and so — ashamed as I am to record the fact — was I. When this truly ghastly woman banged open the door, turned on the top light, and uttered her war cry, "And how are we tonight?" it was all too much. I wanted to say, "We *were* fine," when, without so much as a by-your-leave, out came Polar Bear. Actually, he felt he had his leave — he thought she was the same nurse as the one before.

She was not, of course. I will say this, though, for the sleeping pill monster — she held her ground. But I knew she would not, like the other nurse, let it go. This was strictly a law-and-order nurse. I had to think of something and I tried once again. "They said it was all right" but to say it fell on deaf ears is an understatement. "And who may I ask *us*," she said, looking of course at just me, "is *they?*" The doctor, I said lamely. With that she moved to the chart at the foot of the bed. Oh, not that doctor, I said arrogantly, the head doctor. "Well," she said ominously, "we" — and for the first time not looking only at me — "will see." And with that she started to march out the door.

I tried to continue with the last argument about my "they" but it was no use. She was in such a state of high dudgeon that she had not even remembered to leave me my sleeping pill. And on top of her departure, out came Polar Bear who — I am not making this up — actually put on, for my benefit, if not for hers, a masterful imitation of a cat's idea of a human's high dudgeon.

In any case, it was masterly enough so she did nothing about him, and I never did know whether she tried to do something about him. All I know is that we had one more interruption, which came the next morning. It was the nurse who came to take blood. I was virtually sure Polar Bear would not stand still — or rather lie still — for this, and he did not. But in more than one way it was my fault. For some reason nurses always go for my left arm when they go for blood, and invariably in that left arm they cannot seem to find a good vein to work with. In vain I presented the other arm and begged my visitor to try it but, nurses being nurses, it was no use. After three tries, however, I had had enough. I pulled my left arm away and demanded she try the right one. She refused. We had come to a Mexican standoff — or at least we had one until out from under the covers came my champion. Out he came in full battle stance and, giving the nurse first the hiss and then a growl, he did his masterpiece — he held up a warning paw. It was his right paw, too.

Immediately the nurse knew she was outgunned. Without a word she moved around to the other side of the bed, took my right arm, and took the blood. And even more remarkable, before she left she at least tried a pat in Polar Bear's direction. "I have a cat, too," she said. "I won't say a word."

Later that morning when the men in white came to get us — and some women in white, too — Polar Bear and I went, as the saying goes, quietly.

CHAPTER TWO

My Harvard

Convalescence from being ill is, for most people, very different from the actual illness. But as you certainly know by now I am not most people. Actually, during my convalescent period I wished just as much attention as I wished during my illness. I liked people to gather around my bedside much as they did then, only this time instead of being sad and filled with impending doom I wished them to be congratulatory and filled with admiration for me. And I most certainly did not want them to keep these feelings to themselves. Instead, I wished them to express in their own words how wonderful I had been through all my troubles and how desolate they had been at the thought of coming so close to losing me.

At such times during my convalescence, of course, I liked to take the precaution to warn these people that, on pain of my having a relapse, they must show the same concern they showed when I was ill and be on call twenty-four hours a day. I also said that I thought it was best for them to think of themselves as Army orderlies, always on the ready to bring on the double whatever it was of which at that moment I had the most need — be it food, drink, a book, a magazine, a chess player, or a good conversationalist. If the latter, literally the last thing I wanted was somebody who talked all the time. When I say good conversationalist what I mean is a good listener. There is nothing that ruins a good conversation when you have really gotten going and launched into the subject — and then having the other person turn out to be a rotten listener. I want a person with a good long attention span, and I also want a person who agrees with me. He or she does not have to agree with me right away, but I naturally want him or her to agree with me after I have pointed out the fallacies in their arguments and they have understood the eternal verities in mine.

My assistant, Marian is, I have found over the years, a reasonably good conversationalist for a woman. She is not, however, what I would call — and so few women are — good at arguments. All too often she lacks the basic facts necessary to sustain her side of a question, and completely overlooks the careful marshalling of the facts which I have done on my side. Over the years I have done my best to help her with her logic, but it has not been easy.

Polar Bear, on the other hand, was only an average conversationalist. In the first place, he was far too inclined to be totally concerned with those parts of the conversation which pertained entirely to him — at a cost, obviously, of completely missing other and often far more important parts. In the second place, he could not seem to stretch his little mind into understanding that those parts of the conversation which to him seemed to pertain only to me could well turn out to be important from the point of view of his own deportment and general decorum. And in the third and final place, his attention span was, to be charitable about it, lamentable. The only attention span I can frankly compare it with was that of my second wife, of whom I hasten to add may she rest in peace — something, I assure you, she never gave me.

The reason I brought up the question of the conversational proclivities of Marian and Polar Bear was that I decided that the first trip I was permitted to take after getting ill would be a trip by motorcar to Boston to attend two different reunions — first of my Milton Academy class, and second of my Harvard class. I shall not tell you which number reunions these were because frankly it is none of your business. But they were not yesterday.

Before I was taken ill, Polar Bear detested trips. I really believe, however, that having gotten so used to looking after me during my convalescence, he made the decision that if it was between me going off and leaving him, and him being left behind, or him biting the bullet of a trip, he would take the bullet. Whether or not this is true, the three of us set out by automobile for Boston, and Polar Bear was, if not on his best vehicular behavior, at least not on his worst. Indeed we managed the whole trip with only two stops until we came to Milton, Massachusetts, the town in which the academy is located.

Milton Academy was founded in 1797. My father was partial to any century preceding his own, but he was especially fond of the Eighteenth. Actually, Milton was not the oldest, but it was one of the oldest, of a distinguished group of New England prep schools including Groton, St. Paul's, St. Mark's, and others which, taken together, became known as "The St. Grottlesexers." This was an odd sobriquet because if there was one thing these schools were not long on, it was sex. Only relatively recently did they admit girls at all — not even, in Milton's case, when the girl's school was, literally, just across the street.

What these schools had most in common was that they were extremely strict. One of the things I hoped about going back to the reunion was that I would still find this same strictness as it was in my day, and I felt that just being there and hearing about this strictness could not help but have a salutary effect on Polar Bear's behavior. It is the same way I feel about the behavior of schoolchildren in schools today. They just do what they please, right in the classroom — just the way Polar Bear did just what he pleased, right in the living room.

In any case, as we drove up outside the main building of the school, I could not resist informing both Marian and Polar Bear of what happened to me on my first day at Milton Academy. It was a very memorable day, at least for me. We had a history teacher named Reginald Nash who had been a major league baseball player years before and who was a very dramatic man for a schoolteacher. That day he stood in front of a large map of England with a long pointer in his hand, and he was telling us about a war between England and Holland. "Remember, boys," he said firmly, "this was before the days when England ruled the seas. In those days it was the Dutch who ruled the seas. Why, the ships from Holland even swept right up the English Channel." As he said this he pointed with his pointer to the English Channel on the map, and stared at us like somebody on stage. For some reason his standing there like that and pointing with that pointer reminded me of the picture on a container in the medicine cabinet in my bathroom. Why sir, I said, the Old Dutch Cleansers.

Although the Old Dutch Cleanser container was certainly well known to others of my classmates — and I would have thought that a couple of them would at least have chuckled, if not actually laughed — not a soul did. Instead, the whole room fell ominously silent. Despite all that roomful of new classmates I was left deserted — totally alone. Worst of all, because we were seated alphabetically, I was in the front row, only a few feet from the terrifying Mr. Nash.

Endlessly slowly, it seemed, he put down his pointer. Then, equally endlessly slowly, he took off his glasses and put them on the desk. Next, from his seat only a few feet from me he first delivered one of the longest glares to which I had ever been subjected, and finally, after what seemed an eternity, he spoke. "What," he asked, furiously biting off each word, "is your name?"

Clippie, I replied, supplying my childhood nickname. This sent him into a brand-new second round of fury.

"Your *last* name!" he shouted. Amory, I said. There was now an even longer and more awful silence than the first one. Then once more he spoke. "Master Amory," he said, his voice dripping with sarcasm, "you are, I believe I can say without fear of contradiction, the freshest boy who has ever been at Milton Academy."

I said nothing. "Do you know, Master Amory," he continued, "when Milton Academy was founded?"

Yes sir, I said, 1797. "Good," he said, "then you'll have no trouble studying out exactly how many years, how many classes, and even approximately how many boys you have managed to surpass in freshness since that time." He paused. "Meanwhile," he said, "to accompany you in your study I'm going to give you a far easier number to handle — I am going to give you six marks."

Six marks! I could not believe it. In Milton Academy's marks system one mark was bad enough, two very bad, and three horrendous. But six! I had never even heard of anybody getting that many — and all in one day, and on my very first day. There was only one way you could work off marks. This was by raking leaves Saturday morning — all morning to work off just one mark. My Saturday mornings would be gone until November.

At recess my older brother, who was three classes above me, sought me out. "How's it going?" he asked cheerfully. I told him it was not going very well. "Well," he said, "it's just your first day. Everything probably seems a little confusing. You'll get the hang of it." I told him it was not like that — I just hoped *I* wouldn't be hanged.

At length I told my brother what had happened — that I had been given six marks. "Whew," he whistled. "Six! What the hell did you do, murder someone?" I told him no, but I had made a joke. I then reported the story and the joke to my brother. "God," he said, "it wasn't even a good joke."

My brother was always pretty hard on my jokes. Actually it would not have made any difference if I had made a good joke. Milton Academy was almost a military academy when it came to discipline. The masters taught both with sarcasm and, if necessary, physical punishment. Many a master regularly threw chalk at boys who either talked in his class or fell asleep. And needless to say when the boy stopped talking or woke up it was well understood that he was on no condition to throw it back.

I can remember some of the sarcasm to this day. In that same first year, for example, in the class of a man who later became my favorite master, Al Norris, I whispered something to my friend Vasmer Flint. We often thought we could get away with things in Mr. Norris' class because he wore a green eyeshade and we thought he could not see us very well. Actually, I think he had a magnifying glass in that eyeshade, and his hearing was so acute that it seemed to us that he seemed to be able to hear us even when we just had an idea of talking. At any rate, after my whispering to Vasmer he talked not to me but to the whole class. "Master Amory," he said, "seems to have something of great importance to impart to his friend, Master Flint — something so important it is obviously of far more moment than anything I could possibly be saying. But I hope that Master Amory can be persuaded to part with this information so that the rest of us can be that much more enlightened. I see no reason for it to be reserved to Master Flint alone."

Then for the first time he spoke to me. "Master Amory,"

he said, "if you are not too busy perhaps you will do me the honor of coming up here." As I climbed up to his desk on the platform, Mr. Norris got up from his chair. "Here," he said, "you do not need to stand. Just take my seat. And I hope, if you do not mind, you will permit me to go down and take yours." With that, Mr. Norris and I exchanged seats. Nonetheless, he continued speaking from down there. "Now," he said, "Master Amory, do proceed. Please tell us not only what you told Master Flint but do go on from there. I am sure all of us would like to hear you conduct the class for the remainder of the period."

One thing was certain — after an experience like that, you never again so much as breathed unnecessarily loudly in Mr. Norris' class. But frankly I never thought that being taught with that strictness ever did us the slightest bit of harm. The fact is the majority of us ended up close friends with the masters early on we had feared the most — and furthermore we became friends for life.

Take for example Mr. Nash, the same master who had given me the six marks on my first day. I can remember vividly in the fall of my senior year when he was teaching us another history class at the final class of the day which ran from two o'clock to three o'clock in the afternoon at the exact time when his beloved New York Giants were playing in a World Series game against his detested New York Yankees. Mr. Nash, as I told you, was a former ballplayer and he also coached our baseball team, and he dearly wished at that time not to be teaching his class but to be listening to that game on the radio. Just the same, he knew his duty, and once more he was at his map on the wall and this time in his same dramatic way he was telling us about another war, the late unpleasantness between The States. Once again, too, he had his glasses and his pointer, and he jabbed away at first Vicksburg and then Atlanta. "Grant would make a jab here," he jabbed, "and Joe Johnson would rush to meet him. Then Grant would make another jab over here, and Joe Johnson would once more move to meet that."

Mr. Nash was obviously building to a climax, but suddenly he put the pointer down. Off came the glasses, and finally a long look — right at me. "Cleveland," he said, "the Giants just don't have the power." Almost immediately, however, he caught himself, grabbed his glasses and his pointer, and was back at the map. "And Grant," he went on, "would try again over here but Joe Johnson would get right over there too."

It had taken me six years but it was a long way from those six marks.

Polar Bear was by this time extremely bored with my Milton Academy reminiscences, and was ready to see some action. All reunioners were to be put up right in one of Milton Academy's dormitories. There were younger boys to help us with our luggage, and dutifully Marian and I and Polar Bear made our way to the room to which we had been assigned. I thought the room was very nice and extremely nostalgic, but Polar Bear thought the accommodations were extremely Spartan. He sniffed particularly at the hard chairs. I did not have the heart to tell him I had not had the nerve to tell people I was bringing him. Finally he settled on the bed.

Dinner was to be in the main dining hall with assorted classmates and wives. Obviously, since there was no lock on the door, this presented a problem for Marian and myself with Polar Bear. While we were both looking at Polar Bear and trying to figure out the situation, the same thing suddenly occurred to both of us at once — something we knew, at that moment, was also occurring to Polar Bear. Why didn't we just have room service? Polar Bear is very fond of room service.

Unfortunately, Spartan schools like Milton Academy not only did not have room service, they had obviously never heard of it. Finally, what Marian and I agreed upon doing was having me go downstairs, first to search for some portable food for Polar Bear and, second, hopefully to find some stray classmate who wanted to meet Polar Bear badly enough so that he would be willing to cat-sit for a little while, and thus give Marian and me a chance for a little socializing.

It all worked out, I am glad to say, excellently. I found some food, and also a classmate who agreed to the job. I do not say that Polar Bear took to him, but he took to the food and, afterward, by a general rubbing on his leg, indicated that he would not be adverse to a second helping.

I took advantage of this change for the better from Polar Bear's usual behavior to slip away with Marian and get down to enjoy at least some of the reunion dinner. The first thing I noticed was how terribly old some of my classmates were. Honestly, some of them looked old enough to be my grandfather, let alone one of my classmates. As for the headmaster, he looked like a child. I really could not believe we had been introduced to the right man. All I could think about, when I gradually made conversation with him, was the headmaster of my day — and, frankly, if you thought Mr. Nash and Mr. Norris were tough babies, you never laid eyes on William Lusk Webster Field. He had the largest ears of any man I ever saw. They were like satellites on the sides of his head, and if Mr. Norris could see everything in his classroom, Mr. Field seemed to hear everything, even in other buildings. And if anybody was doing anything wrong in one of those buildings, they were immediately apprehended and brought to Mr. Field. I can still remember from some infraction of my own, standing there in front of Mr. Field at his desk, and seeing nothing but those two enormous ears, which seemed to be reaching out to incarcerate me forever.

Compared to Mr. Field, the headmaster I was talking to could not, at least in my opinion, scare anybody — at least not until he grew up. As for my classmates, when I mentioned to them that I had brought Polar Bear with me, some of them expressed an interest in meeting him or rather, to be accurate, their wives did. My classmates' wives, I quickly learned, were far more discerning readers than my classmates. Immediately, however, I said that I would agree to take any classmate's wife upstairs to meet Polar Bear, or any classmate — provided it was not one who was a member of that original history class who left me to my fate without even a chuckle over the Old Dutch Cleanser. I know as you grow older you ought to let bygones be bygones but there are, after all, some bygones in life that you just simply cannot let be gone.

One classmate's ex-wife turned out to be, of all ironies, my very first girl. Needless to say I made a beeline for her. I had been really crazy about this girl. She was blonde and had pretty bangs and she was none too intelligent, which even then I was smart enough to appreciate. But afterward, when I was away at college or somewhere, she had up and married someone else. It is always discouraging when a girl like that marries beneath you, but what can you do? I put it down to willfulness and a lack of foresight but even that, at the time, did not help much. And even this time, so many years later, I could still remember it well. Indeed, the more we talked over old times the more I sensed how much she felt she had missed, and what a terrible mistake she had made in not marrying me. I could sense these things almost from the beginning of our talk, because I am a very sensitive person.

One of the things we talked about was the days when I was at the boys' school and she was at the girls' school — which I have already told you, and you should have remembered, was entirely separate even though it was just across the street. I discussed with her my opinion that it was far better than this modern nonsense of putting the sexes together before they know the first thing about sex. I went on to tell her all this modern living together had not seemed to improve anything — at least as far as divorce went. At this, to my surprise, she told me she had been divorced three times — which I found shocking, no matter how upset she had been over me. I know I have been divorced twice, but after all I am a man.

I myself took her up to meet Polar Bear. Marian had taken some other people up, too, and a few of them had just gone up by themselves and were introduced to him by the classmate who was looking after him. Actually, Polar Bear could not have been better. He never once retired under the bed or even sulked. And when he looked bored — which he did whenever more than one person approached at once — he did so in a way that was not totally off-putting — which, for him, was really exemplary social behavior. Indeed, during the whole evening he only bit one person, and that was hardly his fault. It was a friend of my first girl's, and the trouble was she had pushed her friend on Polar Bear before he had finished his food — and Polar Bear was never very good before he had finished something. Also, as I have already told you, my first girl was awfully pretty, but to say she was not very bright was being kind.

When it was finally all over and we were retiring for bed, I had to tell Marian and Polar Bear one last story about Milton Academy. This one concerned a catalogue. In my day almost all Milton boys went on to Harvard — at least thirty, and usually more like forty, out of a class of about fifty. When it came to football, Milton's proudest boast of my day was that either eight or nine, I have forgotten which, Milton boys started the Yale game in their senior year at Harvard. I doubt any single high school or prep school ever achieved that record at any time.

Despite these statistics I did not want to go to Harvard. At Milton Academy I had developed certain rebellious traits, and these broke out in full flower in the spring of my senior year. I wrote for catalogues to other colleges. It was just one of those wild crazy flings of youth — you see it today, on a lesser scale of course. In any case, when these catalogues came to me there was one in particular from a college called Stanford. It was located in the West. I was familiar with the West of course — I had an uncle in Dedham and an aunt in Needham — but this particular catalogue was a rather remarkable one. It showed tennis courts and swimming pools. It showed boys and girls studying together — always, as I have said, a doubtful proposition. And finally it showed the young ladies, at least those adjacent to the swimming pools, not by our Boston standards fully clothed.

I was gazing at this catalogue in rapt attention when my father chanced to see it over my shoulder. "Bah," he said.

So I went to Harvard.

On the way from Milton to Harvard I decided to go a roundabout way and show Marian and Polar Bear where I was born — what was then the Boston resort of Nahant. It is now more of a year-round residence, but one thing that has not changed about Nahant is the way it is pronounced. It is pronounced the way the Bostonian pronounces the wife of his uncle, and not what has been corrupted by the rest of the country into a small bug. It is, in other words, Na-*haunt* and not Na-*hant*.

As we drove over the causeway from Lynn into Nahant proper I started looking for the house in which I had been born — which, it is a source of some irritation to me, has never been properly marked. I explained to Marian and Polar Bear that Nahant was in some ways sort of like Milton Academy — it was Spartan and severe. "Cold Roast Boston," it used to be called. A resort, mind you. Just the same, as I also explained to Marian and Polar Bear, we had our good times in Nahant, darn it we did. We had, for example, Dutch-treat picnics. We also had Saturday-night croquet. Then, too, we had swimming. This was at a place called Forty Steps. Like my house, I had a hard time finding this, but I finally did. As we were looking at it, I pointed out to Marian and Polar Bear that to get to the water you had to go down forty steps —

which were not really steps at all. What they were, were rocks. They were slippery and slimy and seaweedy. And, when you finally got down to the water, you did not get to anything like a beach or sand or even pebbles. What you got were more rocks, and they too were slippery and slimy and seaweedy.

As for the water itself, when you got into it, you soon found that it was not just cold water, it was ice-cold water. I put Polar Bear's paw into it to show him how cold it was, and I told both him and Marian that I remember one day when Dad and I were swimming there, among the frigid icebergs, and I suddenly said to him, "Dad, it isn't much fun, is it?" My father turned his by then blue face in my direction. "It isn't meant to be fun," he said. "You feel so good when you get out. What do you want to do — go down on the Cape with the Kennedys?" I told Dad of course I did not want to do that, and I am certain Polar Bear wouldn't have wanted to either.

It is not a long run from Nahant to Cambridge and to Harvard, but Polar Bear went sound asleep anyway, and once we had arrived at Harvard and were ensconced in our reunion rooms, he was quite ready to sleep again. I expected a little more enthusiasm from him seeing, for the first time, his master's alma mater and at least hearing firsthand a knowledgeable history of the oldest college in the country. Honestly, seeing him go right to sleep like that before I had even begun talking made me think how many times in his life he has missed hearing some of my most important thoughts.

Actually, Marian missed some of my words of wisdom too because in no time at all she, like Polar Bear, having located the sofa in the living room, was fast asleep also.

Whereupon, of course, in the time I had before we were to go downstairs to join the reunion lunch I was left alone to think about my life at Harvard. Actually I do not remember whether or not I went to sleep myself and maybe dreamed the whole thing, but in any case there was something about being back in those old college rooms again that took me back to the first time I had entered such a room in my sophomore year.

My roommate then, and in fact for all four years of Harvard, was a Milton Academy classmate. His name was Bruce Foster. Freshman year we had roomed together in what were called "Halls." Next, as sophomores, we were in a "House." Bruce's father, like mine, had been to Harvard and he, like my father, was steeped in Harvard lore. "If a man's in that," Harvard's President Quincy used to say, tapping the Triennial Catalogue, containing a complete list of Harvard graduates, "that's who he is. If he isn't, who is he?" But make no mistake, Harvard's Twentieth Century presidents were equally formidable also. Indeed, of President A. Lawrence Lowell the story is told that a visitor to Harvard seeking to see Mr. Lowell stopped at his office only to be turned away by the secretary, who reported that her boss could not be seen. "The President is in Washington," she said, "seeing Mr. Taft."

One does not need to be a Bostonian at Harvard for long without being willing to concede that in some other cities' societies — New York for one — a certain cachet of social prestige derives from colleges near them — as, for example, Yale or Princeton near New York — but a Bostonian soon learns to attribute this to the fact that such cachet comes from the kind of boy who really belonged at Harvard, but went to some other college due to youthful indiscretion or lack of character. Major Henry Lee Higginson, for example, dedicating the football stadium, Soldiers' Field, which he had given to Harvard, drew this line of condescension as delicately as he could in what was described at the time as one of his "simple, manly addresses." "Princeton is not wicked," he told his audience. "Yale is not base. Mates, the Princeton and Yale fellows are our brothers. Let us beat them fairly if we can, and believe they play the game just as we do."

One thing Bruce and I resolved to do that very first day in our sophomore room was to take easy courses. My reason for this was simple. My brother, during his freshman year, had taken five general courses — four were considered tough enough — and got five straight A's, not even one A minus. He had then also gone on to finish Harvard in three years and gotten a *magna cum laude.* Boston brothers are notably competitive, but for me, as a C student or at best an occasional B, following in the footsteps of such a brother would have been the height of folly without at least trying to level the field.

I had another reason for taking easy courses. Having been editor of the Milton Academy magazine, *Orange and Blue,* I had decided to go out for the *Harvard Crimson* in my sophomore year. But while the *Orange and Blue* was a magazine and came out only once a month, the *Harvard Crimson* was a daily and involved endless evening work, if you did make it, not to mention endless competitions once you did. First there was a competition to be assistant assignment editor, then another to be assignment editor, then a third to be assistant managing editor, a fourth to be managing editor, and fifth and finally a competition to be President. In a nutshell, the amount of time left for your classes was modest indeed.

Bruce, who had no older brother and had not the slightest intention of going out for something like the *Crimson*, had no such excuse. What he did have, however, was something very rare in the Boston and Harvard I grew up in — a well-honed desire to have, during his college years, a grand good time. Bruce was not particularly handsome. He had a kind of narrow face and oversized ears. But he was a very, very funny fellow, and unlike some very funny fellows was enormously good fun to be around. He was as popular with girls as he was with boys, and before he finished at college he was president of the college club and had at least twice as many real friends as the chief class politicians had acquaintances.

Actually the hardest I think I ever saw Bruce work was in our quest to find those easy courses. To begin with we set very high standards, below which we were determined not to go. The first of these was that we would consider only courses which had no examinations. The second was that we wanted courses which met only once a week. Our third criterion was that it must be a course which did not meet before eleven o'clock in the morning. The fourth and final thing we demanded was that the course did not meet above the second floor.

Looking back I realize these last two criteria may seem a trifle picky, but I knew that the *Crimson* would keep me up late many nights, and as for Bruce, his social schedule, particularly in the springtime, was far too heavy for him to consider getting up before eleven. As for the course not being above the second floor, our room was on the third floor, and we got awfully tired of going up and down stairs.

Finally we had our schedules in order. I remember one of my courses was Introduction to Art, and another was Military Science, both of which I had been assured by knowledgeable friends were "pikes" — i.e., easy — and although I had to take one tough course on Chaucer because English Literature was my major, the fourth course Bruce and I came up with was our masterpiece. We really believed we had found the easiest course in the entire Harvard catalogue.

It was called The Idea of Fate and the Gods, a title which did not particularly appeal to us. But as we found out more about it, we were assured by the catalogue that if it was not to be offered that year, the substitute would be The History of Sacrifice, which appealed to us more. And basically either one was, title aside, to our taste close to perfect. There were no examinations, both courses met only once a week, on Fridays from 4 to 6 P.M., and they met on the second floor of the Divinity School. Bruce was a little annoyed that the course met from 4 to 6 P.M. on Friday, because he felt that might interfere with his Friday night dates. But I told him sternly that everything in life which was worthwhile entailed a little sacrifice. I assured him I meant no pun on The History of Sacrifice, but I was certain he would learn something from that, too. Bruce also grumbled a little bit about the Divinity School being a long walk, but I told him if worse came to worst we could take a taxi.

To get into either The Idea of Fate and the Gods or The History of Sacrifice, we soon found out, we would have to be approved by the professor. Dutifully we decided to pay a call on the man. As we walked toward the Divinity School Bruce complained once more about the distance. I told him to look at it this way: at least it was on the level and not up and down, like on the third floor or something.

Once arrived, we learned that the course was given by one of the world authorities on religion, Professor Arthur Darby Nock. Nervously we knocked on his door. Professor Nock himself jumped up and opened it. He looked us over. "What class are you?" he asked. I told him. "Sophomores!" he exclaimed. "Why, I've never even had an undergraduate in The Idea of Fate. I had one in The History of Sacrifice once . . ." he paused, "but we're not offering that this year. Just The Idea of Fate." Suddenly he looked at me. "Foster," he said — he had already mixed us up, and he never did get us straight — "why do you want to take this course?" I looked as earnest as I could. Sir, I told him, all my life I've been interested in the idea of fate and the gods. Professor Nock then turned to Bruce. "Amory," he said, "why do *you* want to take The Idea of Fate and the Gods?" "Same as him," Bruce said, pointing to me. I wanted to kick him. Make up your own ideas, I whisper-hissed to him — he's got us mixed up. Professor Nock was still looking at the papers we had brought him. Finally he looked up. "I guess just because we've never had an undergraduate in The Idea of Fate before doesn't mean we can't ever have one, does it? Or two of them," he smiled. Bruce and I both nodded.

Our first class was a memorable one. The room was filled with graduate students, Jesuit priests, rabbis, and all sorts of people from as far off as Chicago. From the moment Professor Nock began his introduction neither Bruce nor I understood a single word. On top of that, as I say, Professor Nock had mixed us up — a situation which, of course, Bruce immediately latched onto. He started talking to me as if we were not in class at all. "Amory," Professor Nock said, "stop that. You'll have to pay attention here." Bruce, of course, started again. "Amory!" Professor Nock said even more sternly, "I've spoken to you before. I have to have your attention." Again, I whisper-hissed to Bruce. You do that once again, I said, and you will regret it. Needless to say, he did do it again, whereupon I stood up and walked to the door. "Foster! Foster!" Professor Nock said. "Where are you going?" I am going for a walk, sir, I said. I did, too, and I did not return. But Bruce had at least learned his lesson. He did not talk to me in class again. Instead he went almost immediately to sleep.

Toward the end of the term Bruce and I made a very distressing discovery from a fellow classmate. This was in a word that, while there were no examinations in The Idea of Fate and the Gods, there would, however, be a paper due. Furthermore it was a paper whose subject had to be approved by Professor Nock. Frankly, neither Bruce nor I had the slightest idea what we would write about.

Somehow Bruce managed to solve his problem, primarily with the assistance of a friendly minister. But, as my deadline for approval neared, I was getting nowhere. One day, however, in the Chaucer class something happened which rang a bell. What it was, was that I learned that the Chaucer course too would require a paper. To the average person that might not have been anything to solve the problem. But not to yours truly. I rose, if I do say so, to the occasion.

I had, in this Chaucer course, become friends with a

fellow student named J. Sinclair Armstrong — in fact, I was lucky enough to sit beside him because of our Amory/Armstrong juxtaposition. Armstrong later became head of the Securities and Exchange Commission, and as a student he would have been a match for my brother. He took notes in a big, rounded hand which was not only beautiful to see but very easy to copy. One day, shortly after I had copied copiously, I suddenly turned to him. Sinclair, I said earnestly, did Chaucer have much of an idea about the idea of fate and the gods? "Did Chaucer *what?*" Sinclair asked. He looked at me as if I had gone around the bend. No, seriously, I pressed, I really need to know because I have got this little problem. In fact if I do say so, Sinclair, it is now two problems. And there is really no need for it to be any problem at all.

In no time at all Sinclair wormed out of me the whole dastardly scheme I had cooked up — somehow to make one paper of two — both being, of course, Chaucer's idea of fate and the gods, and both being, as I thought of it, a joint effort by Sinclair and me, but unfortunately as Sinclair thought of it, a pretty one-sided thing. At this I took Sinclair into my confidence. I explained to him that I was in a difficult predicament — that I was up against one course that I could not possibly get through without him and another in which I did not understand a single thing. And when it came right down to it, all I was really asking was for him to go through our Chaucer book — I emphasized the "our" to indicate that I felt we were now really a team — and jot down any references which might conceivably concern either the idea of fate or the gods. For him, I said, the whole thing should be a snap. Honestly Sinclair, I promised him, a child could do it.

As I said this I realized I had perhaps gone a little too far. "Well then," he said crossly, "why the hell don't *you* do it?" I reminded him of the *Crimson*, working all night and never getting enough sleep, and still being cheerful with him every morning.

In the end everything worked out fine. The very day I was to give my choice of topic to Professor Nock, Sinclair met me in the morning with a proposed outline. In no time at all I was on my way to Professor Nock. What would he think, I asked him, of a paper on Chaucer's ideas about fate and the gods? He clapped me firmly on the back. "Chaucer!" he said excitedly, "the poet! We've never had a Chaucer. Go to it, Foster." Amory, I said sternly. I told him I thought he would like the idea, and had taken the liberty of preparing a small outline. Actually, I had seen no need to retype it — it was in such beautiful hand-writing. "Beautiful handwriting," Professor Nock said, "beautiful, Foster — I mean Amory. Capital, capital," he said. Then he stopped. "But you understand you're going to have to flesh this out."

I nodded sagely. When I took it back to Sinclair, I told him first the good news — that Professor Nock thought our outline was terrific, and then I gave him the bad news — that he would have to flesh it out a little. Again, at first he was irritated, but in the end he agreed, except this time he would not allow me to hand in his writing. I would have to type it. I told him I thought he was being petty — that we were now a real team, and a team is only as strong as its weakest member.

The final step of course was to convince our Chaucer professor that just what he needed was a paper on Chaucer's idea of fate and the gods. But he fell for it hook, line, and sinker, so again I felt all I should have to do was to carbon a copy for him. There were no Xeroxes in those days. But again Sinclair was difficult and insisted on another typing. I finally, albeit reluctantly, agreed to that also. I have always felt it was important to let employees have a certain say in management. It makes them feel part of the decision-making process, and you never know when you are going to need them again.

There was, finally, an interesting sequel to The Idea of Fate and the Gods. When Bruce and I went to the Divinity School to get back our papers from Professor Nock there, in large letters on both papers, were huge D minuses. This was not good news. For me, it did not mean that I would go on probation, but for Bruce it did. Two C's and two D's was probation. Crestfallen, we went to see Professor Nock to explain the problem. He was his old self. He listened to us for a few moments, then jumped up and grabbed our papers. "Do you know," he said, "I had forgotten all about you being undergraduates?" With that he took a huge crayon, and through the middle of both our D's he drew a line, making them both B's. Then, after looking at them for a moment like an artist examining his painting, he drew two plus signs after them. "There," he said, "two B plusses. Capital, capital." We could not have agreed more.

When Marian woke up we had a consultation about Polar Bear — whether to bring him down to the reunion lunch, in his carrier of course — or whether, as we had done at Milton, get a cat-sitter and then after lunch invite friends who especially wanted to meet him to come up and do so. Unfortunately, however, Harvard had no undergraduates like Milton who were meant to help us old-timers with all sorts of problems, including cat-sitting. So we were finally reduced to the carrier route. All during lunch though we had to keep the carrier under our legs because Harvard's dining room had the usual nonsense about no animals — even for old-timers like myself.

In the old days Polar Bear would not have taken kindly to being at foot level in the carrier, with all sorts of strange people peering down to look at him and pet him. But, as I have said, as he grew older he grew more philosophical about, if not exactly taking what came, at least not constantly making mountains out of molehills. Also, once I had added snacks and even occasional solid food to his social interplay, he decided that being "on," as it were, even on underneath, was not too bad. Indeed, he was clearly enjoying himself when, all of a sudden, there was trouble.

The trouble was in the form of a Harvard house officer of some sort who told me, as if I did not know it, that no animals were allowed in the dining room. I wanted to know if it would be all right if we just shut the carrier top. The young man considered this but finally shook his head. "I'm sorry," he said, "but you're going to have to take him away." When I asked him where — which I did sarcastically — he had no suggestion. In my day, I told him, it was called "Harvard Indifference." I reminded him that we also had a saying, "You can always tell a Harvard man, but you can't tell him much." By this time we were going at it pretty hot and heavy, but for some reason he suddenly eased up. "My sister," he said, out of the blue, "likes cats." I told him I was glad there was someone in his family who did. He ignored this, however, and said that his sister was at the present time handling the coats in the coat room, and if I would take the cat to her he would see that she would handle him through the rest of the lunch.

Marian and I were not keen on turning Polar Bear over to strangers, but the coat room was just a short distance away — enough so we could keep an eye on him — and in short order we could see that not only was Polar Bear doing fine with the difficult man's sister, he was also doing fine with everybody else around the coat room. The woman had opened up the top of his carrier, and we could not believe it when we saw him rising up in there, preening himself, and looking for all the world like a coat room attendant asking for a sizable tip.

Meanwhile, back at our table, the old grads fell, as is their wont, into reminiscing. From the beginning I was amazed at the depth of my classmates' feelings about the good old days in general, and in particular about the good old days at good old Harvard. It was not that I did not understand this — I had seen too many generations at Harvard not to understand — but somehow I was beginning to understand why at Milton I had written for catalogues to other colleges. Finally I felt so out of it that I decided to pull them all up short by reminding them that ''Fair Harvard,'' the Harvard anthem and alma mater, was played at my father's funeral. And, if I do say so, I really think this stopped them. The comedian in the class wanted to know if it was played by the Harvard band. I told him of course it was not — it was played by the regular church organist. At this the wag wanted to know how many verses were played. I told him, naturally, just one verse, but as a matter of fact my father's favorite verse was the last verse, the fourth. I also told him that the words were very memorable, particularly in that fourth and final verse. I added that my mother used to give my brother and myself twenty-five cents for every hymn we learned, and although there was some controversy when my brother chose "Fair Harvard" — I protested that it was not really a hymn — he ended up with twenty-five cents, and so did I. I reminded the class comedian that the words to "Fair Harvard" were written by Reverend Samuel Gilman, and that it was first sung at Harvard's Bicentennial in 1836, and the music was the old Irish folk song "Believe Me, If All Those Endearing Young Charms." If, I added without further ado, I could have the courtesy of some quiet I would be happy to sing it to them. Whereupon I proceeded to do so:

> Farewell, be thy destiny onward and bright,
> To thy children the lesson still give,
> That with freedom to think and with patience to bear,
> And for right ever bravely to live.
> Let not moss-covered error moor thee at its side,
> As the world on truth's current glides by;
> Be the herald of light and the bearer of love
> 'Til the stock of the Puritans die.

I admit I am not the most accomplished of singers but, if I did not get applause, I did at least get a respectful pause. That is, until the class wag had still another question for me. "Are you," he asked, "going to have 'Fair Harvard' sung at your funeral?" I told him I was not, and for two reasons. The first was that although I liked that last verse I did not like that last line, because in my opinion the Puritans were never known as being that big on being bearers of love. The second reason was that I had already decided what I would have played at my funeral — it was the song "Bless the Beasts and the Children."

I told them that "Bless the Beasts and the Children" was Polar Bear's favorite song, too, and I intended to have it played at a memorial service for him someday. That, as I knew it would be, was too much for almost all of them. "A memorial service," the wag said, "for a cat! Now I've heard everything! Are you going to sing it?" I told him I was not going to sing it, but I would certainly have it sung by someone the way I knew not only I would like it best, but also Polar Bear would — with as little emphasis as possible on the word "children" and as much as possible on the word "beasts." Just to be sure they understood what I meant I sang them all that one line, so they couldn't miss it:

Bless the beasts and the . . . 'ildren.

The next most popular subject after Harvard in general at our reunion luncheon was Harvard fund-raising. This topic always seems to loom large at class reunions because Harvard is one very formidable university when it comes to fund-raising. For every class there is a Class Fund chairman, as well as a lot of Class Fund agents who always seem to go to every reunion. These gentlemen point out, in no uncertain fashion, the importance of your giving every year to the Class Fund, and are not above indicating that your last gift was hardly what they would have expected. And, in the event you did not give at all, they make sure you understand how impossible it is for them to meet their quotas when faced with such deadbeats. Unfortunately I am one of these deadbeats. I have not given to my Class Fund for more years than either the Fund or I care to think, because of the simple reason that I have a charity of my own, the Fund for Animals, and this runs counter — at least to my way of thinking — to some things about Harvard I do not like, particularly its treatment of laboratory animals. When I am approached by a Class Fund agent, however, I am always polite and tell them that my late father always gave generously to his Class Fund, my late brother always gave generously to his, and my two nephews both not only give regularly but one of them was at one time actually employed as a fundraiser by Harvard. All in all, I point out, it was hardly a bad show for a family, and he should think of it in the order of something of a record — four and a half out of five.

As for Harvard's record on laboratory animals, however, I found it fell far short. Not long after I had founded the Fund for Animals, one of the first laboratories I visited was Harvard's. I have never forgotten either how difficult they made it for me to enter or what they did once I had done so. Indeed it was something that I have never had happen in any other laboratory I have visited before or since. What they had right with me, besides the usual officials of the laboratory, was a man with a television camera, placed what seemed right behind my neck, literally photographing everything I saw. The idea of this was that if what I would later say was critical — and they could be sure some of it would be — they would have contradictory photographic evidence which would then bolster their usual claim that all the animals were well cared for, had plenty to eat and drink, and were happy. Once upon a time Harvard had leaders who felt differently on the subject of laboratory animals. One such man was none other than Henry David Thoreau, Class of 1837. Mr. Thoreau one day had the misfortune to kill by mistake a turtle which he afterwards decided to send to his friend Louis Agassiz, a scientist at Harvard, to use as a specimen. But, after he did so, Thoreau was extremely troubled, and in his *Journal* wrote as follows:

> I have just been through the process of killing . . . for the sake of science. But I cannot excuse myself for this murder, and see that such actions are inconsistent with the poetic perception, however they may serve science, and will affect the quality of my observations. I pray that I may walk more innocently and serenely through nature. No reasoning whatever reconciles me to this act. It affects my day injuriously. I have lost some self-respect. I have a murderer's experience in a degree.

Thoreau was equally definite in his opinion on the subject when asked in person. Once when asked why he did not shoot birds to study them he replied, "If I wanted to study you, would I shoot you?" On another occasion, asked about college diplomas, he had a memorable reply. "Let every sheep keep its own skin, I say."

It is true that, nowadays, animal activists have finally been able to see that laboratories at least have what is called Animal Care and Use Committees. These are supposed to have at least one member who is not an experimenter but someone who represents the "community," and who can oversee the laboratory's practices objectively. In practice, however, this person is chosen by the experimenters, who regularly rubber-stamp each others' protocols as enthusiastically as they band together to defend each other on the rare occasions they are charged with cruelty. Harvard's Animal Care and Use Committee is typical. It meets only semiannually, and holds its meetings at breakfast in the Faculty Club. An Animal Legal Defense Fund lawyer finally managed to attend one such breakfast. He was not only received with what he reported was "universal hostility," but also found that all members of the Committee were even hostile to the idea of having an outsider, or "community member," present. When the lawyer finally asked if there were any philosophers present, one member of the Committee replied sarcastically, "We're all philosophers here."

Obviously none, sadly, of the stature of Henry David Thoreau. In recent years Harvard appeared front and center in the investigation of research fraud by Representative John Dingell's House Subcommittee on Oversight and Investigation. Indeed, the story of how universities get their grants by first adding everything to their request they can think of — including laboratory rentals, parking spaces, and even cleaning ladies' fees — and on top of that, adding what they call general "overhead," was the crux of the investigation. This was, in almost all cases, over 50 percent of the grant itself. In other words, if a university received a million-dollar grant — to, say, torture cats — they then billed the donor, the National Institutes of Health for example, one million five hundred thousand dollars. Harvard ranked first above all universities in such a practice, coming in at 88 percent, followed by Stanford at 64 percent and Yale at 60 percent.

For reasons I have already made clear I had not, as I said, given to my Class Fund for many years. But, make no mistake, it was not easy. Harvard does not give up on anybody. Year after year they keep after you. And finally, in my case, they produced their crowning achievement. It was in the form of a letter relating to my roommate, the aforementioned Bruce Foster. A Second Lieutenant, Bruce was killed at Kasserine Pass in North Africa in one of the worst disasters of American arms in the Second World War. His unit was maneuvered into a trap by German Field Marshall Rommel, and all but a handful of Americans were killed — Bruce was shot attempting the hopeless task of getting his men out from their crippled tank.

The letter from Harvard about him was, as I say, something of a masterpiece. It was from Laurence Johnson, a friend of mine and the captain of the football team, not even just at Harvard but before that, at Milton. He addressed me by my childhood nickname, as follows:

Dear Clippie:

It has been called to the attention of your Class Committee, several members of whom I know you know well, that you have not for many years made a contribution to our Class Fund. I am sure you understand the pride we have all had in the fact that our class had, last year, the second highest percentage of class givers of any class in recent history — save only the ones who now have only one member left, and, of course, if he goes on giving that class now comes in at 100%. This was hardly a comparison rated against our percentage which happily has a much broader base. We came in, as I said, Clippie, the second highest percentage, based on 92% of givers who we were able to locate.

But Clippie, what I would like to tell you is a story which has nothing to do with numbers or percentages or even regular givers to our Fund. It has to do, on the other hand, with something which I know will have such a deep personal meaning for you that I could not, in all good conscience, let another day pass without informing you.

What it is in a word, Clippie, is that Harvard University has decided to establish a scholarship in the name of Bruce Foster. Bruce was a classmate who you, as his roommate and best friend, undoubtedly remember better than any of the rest of us — and also the memory of his tragic death at Kasserine Pass. I'm sure you know all of this, but what I do not think you know is the remarkable success we have had in our preliminary testing as to the probable success of such an undertaking. In fact, as I write this to you, the sum of $4,500 has already been raised or pledged.

Unfortunately, time is of the essence here because, as again you may or may not know, Harvard does not accept any scholarship under $5,000 and obviously all of us want to go "over the top" before Harvard makes its own decision to let this one go "by the board" — as frankly has been done in the case of many other scholarships.

With this time frame in mind, Clippie, I thought

first of you who would, of all Bruce's friends, want to step forward with a gift which would take care of this matter right now. I knew you would want to do this particularly since the names of a large number of Bruce's classmates who have already given, including Bruce's two sisters, are already known and I am sure you would not like to see any of these read a list of contributors and find you, as Bruce's best friend and roommate, not present.

I'm sure I do not need to say more. All of us here, and especially me, Clippie, await your reply with keen hopes.

Sincerely, your friend
Larry

Marian says I worked longer on my letter of reply than I worked on any other letter or article in her memory. Whether this is true or not, in any case my Class Fund Committee did indeed receive my response. It went as follows:

Dear Larry:

Thank you so much for your letter. You are indeed right that it has been some time since I anted up for my Class Fund. In fact, it has been such a long time that I am embarrassed about it. The problem, Larry, is that I too have a charity, called the Fund for Animals, and any extra money I have I feel should go in that direction, particularly since I have through the years become increasingly unhappy about a conflict between Harvard and the Fund for Animals involving laboratory animals.

I do not want you to be concerned about this, but I do want you to know about it. Now for better news for you. As one who got his feet wet in the field of fund-raising, I yield to no man in my admiration of how Harvard goes about it. Indeed, I believe that anyone entering this field should give his days and nights to a study of how Harvard manages to go on, year after year, raising its millions and even billions of dollars.

Indeed, if I may add a personal observation, I myself have had since graduation hundreds and hundreds of letters from my Class Fund and I sincerely agree that it would be almost impossible to graduate from Harvard and not give to your Class Fund. Sooner or later Harvard will discover, in even the most hard-ened of non-givers, an Achilles' heel, a chink in the armor — something which will in the end mean that they can no longer go on living without changing their non-giving ways. All of us realize such Achilles' heels or chinks do not have to be revealed by the errant non-giver himself, but may come from another person, a more loyal Harvardian, such as a father or mother, a child, a wife, or even a distant relative. But just the same, Harvard will sooner or later find some-one who will bite the bullet, force the issue, and spill the beans.

Larry, I remember a classmate of ours who you too will remember, a man who tried for years not to give to his Class Fund. Finally he got so fed up with re-ceiving letters that he gave up a very successful ad-vertising career, family and friends, chucked it all, and at a very early age moved to the island of Bora Bora.

Here he took up with a dusky maiden and for some time tasted nothing but the fruits of total freedom. And then, suddenly one early part of one memorable evening, just as he and his maiden stood in the doorway of their little grass shack preparatory to going inside for the night she suddenly turned to him and said, "But Don, you haven't given to your Class Fund."

Larry, I cannot vouch for the authenticity of that story but I can indeed believe that our classmate did indeed stop giving up giving, and I feel that I, too, will undoubtedly have to follow in his footsteps.

Larry, what a stroke of genius for you and your committee to come up with a $5,000 scholarship in the name of Bruce Foster, to have Bruce's other friends and even his two sisters know who has given and who has not, and finally to tell me that you have $4,500 already raised, and that Harvard will not accept a scholarship less than $5,000. Really, it's perfect.

Larry, I honestly believe there are few men alive, and even few dead, who could in such a situation avoid bowing to the inevitable. Certainly I do not believe I am one of those men. Indeed I see nothing in the whole unhappy situation but for me to sit down immediately and write you a check for $500.

That was the end of the second page of my letter. I particularly wanted the first part of my letter to him to end at the bottom of a page. I had a feeling that the committee would be sitting around a table, and because of the difficult time they had had over the years with me, they would at least want to hear my letter of surrender read in full. And, when they came to that end of the first part, at the bottom of the page, and heard their chairman read that last line, I could see them all smiling and congratulating each other. I could even see in my mind's eye my old friend Larry pounding the table and saying, "There, I told you! I knew he was tough, but I knew we could get him. There's a way — there's always a way!"

Next I knew, however, they would have to turn the page. That was because I still had remaining my Page Three:

Larry, you just had one terrible piece of luck. Do not please think it will ever happen again, and don't on any condition reassess your strategies. They are good strategies, in fact they are close to perfect. Larry, the bad luck is simply that you got me.

Larry, I am not going to send you my check for $500 — in fact, I am not going to send you a check at all. I simply cannot. Bruce loved so many things about Harvard. He loved the friends he made. He loved where he lived, both in his Hall freshman year and in sophomore and ensuing years in the House. He loved luncheons at the club, afternoon sports, evenings walking on the Charles River, and looking for feminine company.

But there was, Larry, just one thing Bruce did not like about Harvard. He did not like the books. He did not like the books or the studying. He knew how to stay off probation — that he needed three C's and a D — but, once when he received four C's, he was very angry. He felt he had obviously over-studied.

Larry, I do not need to give you more examples. It

is unnecessary. For you to give a scholarship for such a man would be a blot on the escutcheon of Harvard forever. You and the committee would go down in Harvard history as the Committee of Sham and Shame. You would indeed have made a mockery of Harvard's own motto of "Veritas."

I realize that I have left you with a problem. You have $4,500 raised, and Harvard will not accept $4,500. What can you do? Larry, I have an idea. I note there are nine members of your committee. Forget the scholarship. Each one of you should take $500, get yourself a plane ticket, go to Las Vegas, and have yourself a hell of a weekend. Bruce would have loved that.

Sincerely, still your friend,

Clippie

If I do say so, for a long time I was not bothered by any more letters from our Class Committee. The class did, however, put on one memorable happening at the time of our Twenty-Fifth reunion. Harvard is very big on Twenty-Fifth reunions. For your Twenty-Fifth and Twenty-Fifth only, the entire class gets to go back with their families and spend time in the hallowed Halls and the Houses. As a member of the Twenty-Fifth you are even more important than the Oldest Living Graduate. Indeed, many people now feel that the whole Oldest Living Graduate competition is not what it was in the old days — that it is not, to be blunt about it, played the way it was meant to be played. Nowadays there are Oldest Living Graduate candidates who take practically no chances at all and hardly ever leave their room.

Fortunately such goings-on have never taken place in Twenty-Fifth reunions. The competition to give Harvard more money than any previous Twenty-Fifth class is fierce, but the game is played absolutely fairly and squarely.

Indeed the Twenty-Fifth is such a huge event that before our Twenty-Fifth reunion even started all the members of the class from New York, New Jersey, and Connecticut were invited to a dinner at the Harvard Club of New York. Here we would all be addressed by none other than the President of Harvard himself, Dr. Nathan Marsh Pusey.

Dr. Pusey did an extraordinary job in his talk. He told us all about the new Harvard we would shortly be seeing when we journeyed up to Cambridge for our reunion. And it was not an easy job, either. Many members of the class had, as in the good old days, entered their sons at birth to Harvard — and now even their daughters — and a large number of them had not gotten in. Clearly, Dr. Pusey's most difficult job was explaining to those parents of those children why they had not made it.

But, as I say, there was no question that Dr. Pusey was up to the task. He explained exactly what the new Harvard was. He explained the way, for example, Harvard scoured and scouted for new Harvardians all over the world. They would, for example, find one fellow in Tierra del Fuego, and maybe another in Madagascar, and possibly a third in Reykjavik, and on and on, until they had brought dozens and dozens more to Harvard to study. And Dr. Pusey went on to explain that these new students would not necessarily graduate as we had done — they would just stay on, and get M.A.'s and Ph.D.'s, and so on. But, he assured us, we would not be neglected, either. We would have the honor of supporting them — year after year. We actually would have the chance, at this reunion alone, Dr. Pusey went on, to give Harvard more money than any previous returning Twenty-Fifth class had ever given it.

Honestly, after that, we all felt terrible about the very idea of entering our own sons or daughters. All they could do was drag the place down.

It was almost over. Before it was, however, Dr. Pusey made one mistake — he asked for questions. But it was not really his fault. It was just one of those things that happened. What happened was that a classmate of ours, a man whom Dr. Pusey could not have known, rose to his feet at the back of the room.

Our classmate is a man who came over on the Mayflower, and frankly he has not done a great deal since. He has tried a lot of things, like selling stocks and bonds to his friends, or selling them insurance, or even automobiles, but what he really found he was best at was doing nothing. He is the kind of fellow who is very good at weekends but not very good in the middle of the week. He is, as I say, really a very nice fellow, but the plain fact is after seven o'clock in the evening he gets increasingly perilous. At lunchtime, at five o'clock, or even possibly six o'clock, Dr. Pusey could have asked for questions with him in the audience with no trouble at all. It would have been fine. But at nine o'clock it was far from fine.

Slowly our classmate rose to his feet and wove his way to a nearby microphone. Actually, for nine o'clock we thought he was doing very well, but of course we were used to him. "Dr. Pushy," he said, "I have a ques-shun. Whaddya gonna do about a fellow who came over on the Mayflower, and his shun went to Harvard, and his shun went to Harvard, and his shun went to Harvard . . ." Obviously our classmate was going to keep on through all the eleven generations his family had indeed been to Harvard. We did not want to stop him. All of us already knew if you tried to stop him you only got into more trouble. Slowly he intoned on, ". . . and his shun went to Harvard, and his shun went to Harvard, and his shun went to Harvard . . ." And then, at last, he concluded, ". . . and his shun can't get into Harvard. Whaddya gonna do about that, Dr. Pushy?"

To Dr. Pusey's everlasting credit, the silence was mercifully brief. He rose to his feet. "I don't know what we're going to do about it," he said. "We can't send him back. The Mayflower doesn't run any more."

CHAPTER THREE

First Jobs

Polar Bear was not a party animal. Actually, I never had a party which he even remotely appeared to enjoy. And when I say even remotely, I mean just that — he was usually under the bed or the sofa or in a closet.

For one thing, he was severely lacking in small talk — surely a part and parcel essential for any party. I often described him as terrific at vowels, but terrible at consonants. His AEIOU's, for example, might waken a wake, but they were hardly even passable party fare. When toned down they made a fine hello, and I have always believed they would work well on a telephone answering machine, although I never had any luck in trying to teach Polar Bear how to do this. But the trouble was, for a party these AEIOU's of his always seemed to have to do with him only, and nobody and nothing else — hardly a party plus. As for his attempts at genuine MEOW's, these were almost totally lacking in being a party asset. Indeed, because of the lack of an "M" in his vocabulary, they were hardly distinguishable from one of his gentler AEIOU's.

All in all, when there was a party invariably the cat seemed, if Polar Bear would forgive the phrase, to have gotten his tongue. He simply did not have that prime of all party essentials — the gift of gab. He did not either open a conversation, keep a conversation going, or even, for that matter, contribute to its graceful conclusion.

There was something else that Polar Bear lacked when it came to parties. Years ago my grandmother used to say that the trouble with the younger generation was that they had never been taught not to "look out loud." Her generation, she maintained, was always taught that, and was brought up on the idea that if they could not smile and say something pleasant, they could at least smile and think something pleasant and above all, as she put it, not "look out loud."

Frankly, Polar Bear was awful about not looking out loud. And it was not that I did not try to teach him not to do it, either. I did — but it's not an easy thing to teach — especially when he is looking out loud at you all the time and you are the one doing the teaching. And, make no mistake, when he looked out loud, it was not just a minor look out loud, it was a major, and where a party was concerned it was invariably critical. In fact, he almost invariably made a whole critical analysis of both the people, and what they are doing, and, worst of all, a totally unfavorable opinion of why they were there in the first place.

I really believe Polar Bear enjoyed working on his critiques long before the party began. Somehow he always seemed to know days ahead when there was going to be a party. Whether this was because of the extra goings-on in the apartment, the extra cleaning, the scurrying around in the pantry or the kitchen, or whatever, he somehow always knew. And, from that very moment that he knew, he had the very opposite of the good party-giver's desire to make a party go. He wanted to make the party stop.

He had, it is true, his side. For many years he made no secret of the fact that he had already met everyone he wanted to meet, and indeed, as a matter of another fact, he would like to subtract a by no means small number of those. In latter years, as I have pointed out, he was somewhat better, but whether this was just because his attitude years ago could hardly have been worse, or whether I had just gotten more used to it, or whether I was clutching at straws, I really did not know.

But one thing I did know — I never allowed this antisocial side of him to stop me from enjoying having my friends over — and this even though, in the early days at least, I paid dearly for it. When, for example, a large party was about to begin and the cook was about to begin cooking, and the caterer was about to begin catering, Polar Bear would immediately sink down and skulk and mope around as if he were an armadillo on his last legs. And when I would go to him to try to cheer him up it was no use. He gave me, in spades, that look my grandmother so disliked, and to say it was not out loud is an understatement. It was in fact out very loud — all the way from his half-shut eyes to his droopy tail. He made even his whiskers look bedraggled, and as for his nose, it was unmistakably sniffing around as if to smell something about to expire. All in all, every inch of him proceeded to give me warning that if I proceeded on with my idea of the party I might very well find him not only at death's door in the morning but very possibly actually through the door.

This is not to say that in my by no means large New York apartment I was constantly throwing parties. I would just try, as other people do, to reciprocate, and when friends had you over for cocktails, a lunch, a dinner, or whatever, you naturally wanted to do your best to return the favor. Actually I gave only one large party a year, which I have come to call my Marathon Party. I hasten to state that this was not a marathon party in the sense of size, even if it was somewhat in the sense of length. Actually the party begins when anybody wants to come. The New York Marathon begins on television in the late morning, and you see about twenty-five thousand or more runners starting out, jammed along the Verrazano Bridge. It then goes on until finishing time which, for the winners, is shortly after two o'clock, but for the stragglers goes on until late in the afternoon. Actually the finish is only a hundred yards or so from my apartment, and the runners having gone once around Central Park come down Central Park South and then finish around the corner. Since my apartment has an eighth-floor balcony, it is really a terrific place to see the race and, since Polar Bear had his own wired-in balcony just beside the main balcony he too could watch it all, were he in a party mood. Suffice it to say that I have had at least eight marathon parties and I cannot remember a single one of them for which he was in what I would call a party mood.

This was particularly galling to me because Polar Bear could well go out on his own balcony via the bedroom window and watch the marathon and not be bothered by a single guest who could not reach him there. The main balcony, you see, was reached by the door, and Polar Bear's was entirely wired as a safety measure from (1) his jumping off it, and (2) for pigeons. It was really a masterful piece of design by me which to my mind was not nearly as appreciated by him as it should have been — particularly since it was really only one day a year he had a constant stream of people standing out there beside him. At such a time it seemed to me he never even stopped to think that the whole rest of the year he could go out on his side of the balcony and sit and think in solitary satisfaction.

As usual my party was a mixture of old men friends and new girlfriends. No, I am joking of course. But it was a mixture of old and new friends — not to mention friends of friends. In other words, friends who brought friends. This is a typical New York habit — despite the fact that New Yorkers probably have on average fewer house guests, whom they would at least have an excuse to bring, than any other city in the country. In other words, they bring to you guests they would not think of asking to stay with them.

For this Marathon Party I made a special effort to include many people Polar Bear knew particularly well. And I also included several people who had never been to my Marathon Party before and yet were people I particularly wanted Polar Bear, if he would deign to do so, to meet. Not the least among these were Mr. and Mrs. Primo Acernese, from Allentown, Pennsylvania. I had met Mr. Acernese under perhaps as unusual circumstances as I can ever remember meeting anybody. It took place in the early morning at Hegins, Pennsylvania, the site of the country's most infamous annual live pigeon shoot. Because of this particular shoot's country-wide publicity and egregious cruelty, the Fund for Animals had decided both to try to get as many animal activists as possible to the scene, and also to hold there the day before our annual national conference, one normally held in a more civilized location.

One thing was certain about the shoot. Although there would be hundreds and hundreds of animal activists from all over the country bravely opposing it, there would be thousands and thousands of local yokels violently supporting it. As for the thousands of trapped pigeons, most of them were pen-raised and, feeble from lack of food and water — many having never flown before — they were so disoriented that when suddenly released from the traps in front of the line of shotgunners they often did not fly at all, but just unsteadily walked out of the traps. They were then blasted on the ground, literally only a few feet from the feet of the gunners. Around the shooters were the so-called "trapper boys." These are local kids who put the pigeons into the traps and release them by pulling the string attached to the trap when the gunners say "Pull." They are also supposed, in between the shooting, to break the necks of the wounded pigeons, but there are so many of these wounded that the boys often do not bother to break their necks but simply throw them into trash cans hidden from the crowd behind wooden screens. The lucky birds, in other words, have their necks wrung. The unlucky ones either bleed to death or otherwise die slowly and painfully.

Even the attempt to stop such sadism — for which some 250 shooters pay as much as $450 — would not, we knew, be easy particularly when it would all take place in one of the cruelest states in America. Indeed, of the Pennsylvania Game Department I had said many times that they would shoot their mother if she was on four legs. I had not yet seen the pigeon shoot when I had said that but after seeing it I felt that I was perhaps doing a disservice in not counting the shooting of mothers who had only two legs. Actually the area, we learned, would be patrolled by, besides the Pennsylvania Game Department, 170 State Police.

About one o'clock the night before, when Wayne Pacelle, our National Director, and I were discussing last-minute plans, my telephone rang. It was a longtime friend of mine named Syndee Brinkman, former head of the National Alliance for Animals, who wanted to come over right away. She had, she said, a special request. When Syndee arrived she told me that she had heard that some of the shooters were, as she put it, "out to get me," and would I be willing to get myself a bodyguard? She said she already had the man and that he was home, waiting for a phone call.

I should point out I told her that I had never had a bodyguard before and that I was neither a gangster nor a President and, furthermore, I did not believe in guns. Syndee is not a woman who takes no for an answer and, unknowingly, I had given to her a foothold. "This one I am thinking of," she told me, "doesn't use a gun. He runs a martial arts school and he's a God knows what degree black belt Cheonkido. That's beyond Taikwondo," she added.

I had never heard of Cheonkido or Taikwondo but I must admit I was intrigued. I was once a boxer, but now with arthritis and some other problems I had no desire to be mugged by the kind of person who would torture a pigeon. Her idea, I admitted, might be an interesting way to handle the thing. Meanwhile Wayne, an old friend of Syndee's, checked in firmly on her side. He asked Syndee to demonstrate what her man could do — whereupon Syndee said that she herself had held a board over her head, full stretch, and that from a standing start her man jumped up, hit the board with both feet, and broke it.

I told her I hoped she knew I did not want him to kill anybody, but I was too late. Syndee was already on the phone, telling Mr. Primo Acernese to meet us at the pigeon shoot. She then handed the phone to me. I expected at the least gruffness, but I soon realized the man whom I was talking to was a soft-spoken gentleman.

The next morning when I met him I was surprised again. I expected a large, powerful fellow with bulging muscles. Primo was small — about five foot six — slight, and weighed less than 150 pounds. He seemed to have no bulging muscles at all. Very soon I was to notice, however, that wherever you touched him he was hard as a rock. Actually the most suspicious thing I could see about him was that he was wearing dark glasses.

"You tell me where you want to go," he said quietly, "and I'll tell you whether you can go there or not." Suddenly I felt like a prisoner, or at least someone guarded by the Secret Service. I told him I wanted to see everything, and I wanted to start by going over to the shooting line. Without a word he went ahead in that direction and I followed him. "But when I want you to go somewhere else," he said over his shoulder, "you go immediately."

We did not have long to wait. As we approached the shooting line I noticed three men moving in my direction. "There's the guy," one of them said, "Let's get him right now." Primo had stopped and so did I. As the three men approached, however, Primo did not seem to be doing anything but watching them. Then he turned to me. "Over there," he said quietly, "in front of that wall." I looked where he wanted me to go. "Now," he said, this time less quietly. Why there, I wondered. This time I did not get any answer, but just a shove toward the wall. I later learned that Primo did not mind how many people were in front of me, but he did not want anyone behind me.

The approaching trio were now almost on top of us. I noticed how much larger they were than Primo. Suddenly Primo moved forward just a step. "Stop," he said quietly. Equally suddenly the men stopped in their tracks. I could not hear what else Primo said to them, but it was my impression that he had not said anything. They had just decided, on closer inspection, that there was something about him that made it clear to them that for them to do anything more was not going to be either profitable or healthy.

All day it was like that — anyone who approached who was not a friend never came beyond where Primo wanted them. Meanwhile, the appalling shoot went on. Despite the efforts of the animal people, who were kept from the shooters by the police, thousands of birds were shot. Nonetheless, the brave activists who broke through the lines were successful in rescuing some 500 birds — after which, of course, they were carried off to jail in buses. On the last bus of the day, clearly visible on the roof of the bus was one of the pigeons.

Once during the day I asked Primo if he wanted a Coke. "I never drink when I'm working," he said. Finally at the end of the day when I demanded he take some money for his work he shook his head. I started to press it on him, completely forgetting myself and by now totally confident. I told him kindly to remember that I was bigger than he was. For the first time all day he smiled.

Polar Bear never thought very much of a party which started before lunch. But since this one did, he at least expected it to end at a reasonable hour. This, however, was obviously not happening either. He then did something quite unusual for him — he made the best of it. He did this by responding to Primo and his wife, Carol, even though they were both obviously dog people. And if there was one thing Polar Bear well knew it was that there was a large difference between dog people and cat people. But he also seemed to know right away that although Primo and Carol might have had dogs, they were not just dog people — they were cat people, too, and in fact they were animal people in general. A good example of this, as Carol told us, was that both their dogs were strays — a huge Doberman type named Bill, and a tiny little guy named Fido of, she said, extremely uncertain origin. Who was the boss? we all wanted to know. "Fido, naturally," said Primo firmly. We also all wanted to know if Carol worried when Primo was either out guarding or competing with advanced students. Carol shook her head. "No," she said, "because he's so good at it." What if, we insisted, he was against someone as good as he was? "He wouldn't be," she said quietly, "and if it turned out to be that way, Primo would figure out what to do."

The next person who had never been to my Marathon Party before and whom I especially wanted Polar Bear to meet was a man named William Zinsser — with whom I went all the way back to my college days. I had, as a sophomore, applied at the Harvard employment office for a summer job as a tutor-companion. These jobs still exist today, but they have become more of a female pursuit — basically governessing young children. In my day the pursuit was primarily male. The boys we were to look after were older — Bill, for example, was fourteen — and despite the description "tutor-companion," few of these jobs involved any tutorial work. Instead, the operating word was "companion." You looked after your charge to the extent that you drove him around, saw that he got in on time if he was out at night, and during the day you played outdoor sports with him — tennis, golf, sailing, etc. — as well as, in the evening, a wide variety of indoor games. As for pay, I was to get a hundred dollars a month and a fifty-dollar bonus if I did a good job. I was not going to get rich on my first job, but I did have free board and lodging and no expenses, and for those days it was considered good pay and the jobs were extremely desirable.

When Bill and his wife, Caroline, came in and were introduced all around, particularly to Polar Bear, I suddenly realized looking at Bill that to me he was still fourteen and I was about eighteen or whatever I was then.

There is something about age differences so pronounced in those days they seem to stay that way when you suddenly go back to them. Actually a four-year spread, when you are both in your fifties or sixties, is meaningless, but when you are fourteen and eighteen it is a huge differential. I even had difficulty thinking of him as the distinguished author he had become. Indeed, after many years as a writer and editor on the old *New York Herald Tribune* and as a highly successful teacher of writing at Yale, he had produced one of the all-time classics about writing, called *On Writing Well*. But none of that would have been possible, I told everybody firmly, had I not rescued him from the shellac business where, when I first knew him, he seemed to be headed because his father was the owner of a shellac company.

This was not exactly true, of course. My stories in such circumstances, when I have a large audience, rarely are. Actually, Bill could not understand the first thing about chemistry, and he would have been a menace in the shellac business. It was his mother who had the literary inclinations that were later translated into his career. Nonetheless, I not only took credit for it all, I went on to describe, in glowing terms, my first night on my first job. It was, to say the least, a nightmare of an experience.

I should explain that Bill and I were in a third-floor room. Later, when his mother and father as well as his two older sisters went abroad, we would have separate rooms. In any case, like most college-aged students, I was sleeping incredibly soundly when all of a sudden, still three-quarters asleep, I felt a toe being tickled. Promptly I pulled my leg up under me. Somehow, though, the toe was found and the tickling continued. By now only half asleep, I realized that someone was doing this tickling, and I was focused enough to figure out that if this was Bill, I would have to take stern and immediate steps to discourage such behavior. And stern steps were just what I did take. Without further ado I pulled both my legs still further up under me and with both feet lashed out at the intruder.

Immediately I heard first a deep and ominous groan and, then, a tremendous crash. At this I woke up completely and to my horror saw Bill's father sitting on the floor, clutching his stomach — which of course I had effectively karated. For a moment neither of us spoke. I had at least started mumbling apologies, but even these were interrupted by his gruff explanation. "The telephone is for you," he said. "Whoever it is says it's very important. You'll have to come downstairs. The telephone is in our room."

As Mr. Zinsser led the way down the narrow stairs I again made apologies which now, after looking at my watch and seeing that it was exactly 2:30 A.M., I put into high gear. But the worst was yet to come. The telephone turned out to be right by Mr. and Mrs. Zinsser's bed. Indeed, it was right by Mrs. Zinsser's head. "Hello," she said politely, holding the phone up toward me. Once more I apologized and seized the instrument.

"Clippie!" a voice shouted, a voice which to my horror came from someone at least three sheets to the wind. I tried to hold the phone as high as possible — with one hand over the earpiece to cover the sound of his voice — but I did not believe I was totally handling this situation. I could only hope that the message from an old Milton classmate of mine, R. Bennett Forbes, Jr., was not getting through either to Mrs. Zinsser or to her husband, who had retired on the other side of the bed.

What this message was, in a word, was that Bennett was at a debutante dance at the Seawanhaka-Corinthian Yacht Club in Oyster Bay and he had learned, through my brother, who was teaching sailing there for the summer, that I had a job at the Zinssers' house in nearby Great Neck. The party was absolutely terrific according to Bennett, a connoisseur of such affairs.

Finally his voice stopped. In as even and serious voice as I could muster, and one that, considering my situation, would have done credit to learning of a death in the family, I stated firmly, entirely for the Zinssers' benefit, that then there was, Ben old boy, nothing I could do about it until the morning, was there?

This was of course a major mistake because it immediately sent Bennett off into a paroxysm of rage. "No, no, no!" he shouted while I earnestly pushed the telephone towards the ceiling. "Not in the morning — now! Hell, it's not even three o'clock!"

At this point I gave up. Don't worry, I repeated in the same voice in which I had earlier attempted to do the job, I'll call you first thing in the morning. With that, firmly, I hung up. I had taken a terrible chance that he would call back, but for the first time in the whole nightmarish experience I got a break and he did not. Before leaving I told the Zinssers that I was terribly sorry about the emergency — a word I had some difficulty with but which I nonetheless gamely tried — and said good night.

The next morning there was a postscript to the episode. At breakfast neither Mr. nor Mrs. Zinsser made any mention of the telephone call that night to the rest of the family.

But when we were all assembled at the dining room table, Mrs. Zinsser, who liked to give out the mail at breakfast and who made some ceremony of it — for which in this case I could hardly blame her — slowly passed a postcard addressed to me which at least two of the elder Zinsser sisters, as they took it on the way to me, could hardly avoid seeing. "This," Mrs. Zinsser said, "seems to be for you." It was indeed. "Mr. Cleveland Amory," the address said, "C/o Mr. And Mrs. William Zinsser, Great Neck, Hot Dog, Long Island."

It was of course from Bruce — and it somehow made a fitting end to my first twenty-four hours of trying to make my living in a cold, cruel world. Actually the job itself, as it developed, had both bad and good points. The first bad point was that when Mr. and Mrs. Zinsser and the two elder sisters went abroad, Bill and I and another sister did not stay in their house but went to Bill's grandmother's house. The second bad thing was that the grandmother had lived alone in that house, albeit with several servants, for a quarter of a century. Indeed, she was as set in her ways as any older woman I have ever known — and I have known my share. The third bad point was that the aforesaid servants of said grandmother were almost as set in their ways as their mistress and, besides, they took the view that whatever a tutor-companion was, it did not belong upstairs or at the family dining room table. It belonged below stairs with them, and should eat there as well. As for making my bed, they just did not do it. I made my own bed the entire summer.

The good point of the job was that however tough the grandmother and the servants made life for me, Bill and his sister June made up for it. If their grandmother criticized me for anything — and she did a great deal — they both took my side immediately. Indeed, sometimes they went well beyond the bounds of taking my side. I remember one day when their grandmother had lost her glasses. First at the table she asked June where her glasses were. June said she did not know. The grandmother next turned to Bill. When Bill did not know either, it was my turn. "All right, Mr. Amory," she said, as if I was already identified and convicted as the perpetrator, "will you please give me my glasses?" This was too much for Bill. "Oh, Grandma," he said, "I suppose every time Mr. Amory loses his baseball he says, 'All right, Mrs. Zinsser, give me my baseball.' "

The use of the word "baseball" — before tennis ball or any other kind of ball — was natural. Bill and I enjoyed sailing and tennis and golf and swimming, but our first love was baseball. Almost every evening we went out and had a catch or hit flies or grounders to each other, and indeed it was not long before we came naturally to a joint invention of what, if I do say so, was the very best two-man baseball game ever invented.

I know there have been many other two-man baseball games invented over the years by men and boys — and even nowadays I suppose the occasional one by girls — but I repeat, ours was the best. To begin with, we not only invented it on a tennis court, we played it on a tennis court. We did play our share of tennis — I was on the tennis team at school, and part of my job was teaching Bill tennis — which was not difficult because he was a very good player. But at baseball he was even better, and so, frankly, was our game.

In the back of the court, attached to the fencing, we

placed a rectangular board which defined the strike zone. Directly in front of it we placed a home plate. We then marked a pitching rubber just inside the net. When the pitcher hit the wood it was a strike — the wire, a ball. A line drive over the net, but not far enough to hit against the fencing at the other side of the court, was a single. A line drive which hit the far back fencing was a double. If it hit either the far left or the far right fencing, it was a triple. If it went entirely out of the court it was a home run.

There were several other refinements we made which I know all you fans are anxious to hear. A grounder, for example, hit toward the pitcher and fielded by him had to be either thrown over a bag we placed at first base or if picked up, the pitcher could run over and tag the runner before he got to the bag. If the pitcher caught a line drive and there was someone on base, it was a double play.

Of course I have given you just the bare outline of the game we invented. And remember we did not play just against ourselves — we played a whole team against another whole team. We knew the names of all the players on all the major league teams by heart, and whether they were right-handed batters or left-handed batters. If you had a left-handed batter you had to bat left-handed. The only exception we made was if you had a left-handed pitcher you did not have to pitch lefty. We tried it over and over, but we just could not get the damned ball over the plate well enough.

When it came to us being individually a whole team, we did have some arguments. Since Bill went to Deerfield and was reasonably Massachusetts he wanted to be the Red Sox and so, of course, did I. And we both of course detested the Yankees. What we did when we had to have them in a Series against each other was to ration them in reverse. In other words, if you had had them not long before, you did not have to have them. And we were very tough on the other guy for not trying when he had the Yankees. We had some terrible rows about that.

Sundays we always played doubleheaders. I will never forget one we had when I played the Red Sox against Bill's Detroit Tigers. Bill had Schoolboy Rowe and Tommy Bridges as pitchers, Mickey Cochrane as catcher, an infield of Hank Greenberg, Charlie Gehringer, Billy Rogell, and Marv Owen, and an outfield of Goose Goslin, Pete Fox, and Al Simmons. Meanwhile I met him with Wes Farrell and Lefty Grove pitching, Rick Farrell catching, an infield of Jimmy Foxx, Eric McNair, Joe Cronin, and Pinky Higgins, and an outfield of Heinie Manush, Doc Cramer, and Mel Almada. It was dark when we finished and everybody up at the house was yelling, but we kept on anyway and would have finished both games if we had not lost the last ball we had.

Of course our games took a toll of the tennis court. Finally, when the battering we gave the fencing behind home plate was too much we prevailed upon the gardener to fix it after carefully explaining to him what an honor it was to be the head of a grounds crew for a Sunday doubleheader. We also explained to him how important it was for him always to bring his dog, because his dog was really terrific at going after home runs.

I think one of the reasons Bill was so intrigued with Polar Bear was that in his classic book on writing, he devoted in his chapter on humor a large section on *archy and mehitabel*, by Don Marquis. "No formal essay, for instance," he wrote, "could more thoroughly deflate all the aging actors who bemoan the current state of the theater than Marquis does in 'the old trouper,' a long poem in which Archy describes Mehitabel's meeting with an old theater cat named Tom:

> *i come of a long line*
> *of theatre cats*
> *my grandfather*
> *was with forrest*
> *he had it he was a real trouper . . .*
> *once he lost his beard*
> *and my grandfather*
> *dropped from the*
> *fly gallery and landed*
> *under his chin*
> *and played his beard*
> *for the rest of the act*
> *you don t see any theatre*
> *cats that could do that*
> *nowadays*
> *they haven t got it they*
> *haven t got it*
> *here . . .*

Intrigued as Bill was with Tom, he had to admit that Polar Bear was more of a Mehitabel. Polar Bear, no anti-feminist, took this sexual transformation with, I thought, extremely good grace. As for myself, I still had another story to tell my guests. What happened was that many years later, looking back at being a tutor-companion as such a curious but interesting job, I ended up deciding to base a television series around the idea, or at least this is the way I thought of it in retrospect. Actually what happened was that I had a meeting with Douglas Cramer, the then director of TV programming for the ABC Television network. Mr. Cramer asked me if I had an idea for a television show. I told him I did. He wanted to know what it was. I said what it was, was to have a show called "Saturday Review," a real magazine of the air, one which would handle the arts, movies, theater, books, even television itself. Mr. Cramer said he had an idea, too — it was to have a show based on my writings in the field of Society.

So we compromised. We came up with an idea based on my writings in the field of Society. Actually, this was where my second idea, the story of the tutor-companion, came in. And as the idea took shape it was very exciting. Soon I had written the introduction for a treatment of the show, as follows:

Once upon a time, I wrote — such as the TV season of 1965–1966 — there was a lovable old millionaire from Oklahoma named O.K. Crackerby, a man with a fortune in, in more ways than one, natural gas. He is a widower with three children (an older girl and two younger boys), a man who has come East to ply the Eastern resort circuit, since he promised his "missus," before she passed on, that some day he would stop just making money and do right by the kids. To do this, to make little gentlemen out of the little monsters, and out of the girl a "debbytant," he has acquired the services of something he has learned the Eastern resort families have — a "tutor-companion." The latter would be the star —

the man whose job it would be to teach the kids there is something more in the world than making money. He would teach them manners, how to play sports and, perhaps most important, how to be a good sport. Above all, the show would not only have the conflict between *nouveau riche* and *ancien régime* — it would also have, as a dividend, an ever-changing lush background of this country's great resorts.

Mr. Cramer leaped at it all, especially at the tutor-companion idea — and particularly the name I had chosen for the young man, St. John Quincy, pronounced "Sinjin Quinzy." In fact, everyone at ABC was so taken with the idea of a brand-new character in a job which nobody in Hollywood had ever heard of that they decided to forgo calling the whole show "O.K. Crackerby!" as I had — instead they decided to call it "My Man St. John."

In any case, soon the treatment was completed and the show went onward and upward to the final board meeting where the ultimate summit decisions are made. They are really thrilling, those final meetings. In a big room around a large table sit all the top network brass — Mr. Leonard Goldenson, the president in charge of all the other presidents, Mr. Thomas Moore, the president in charge of all the other presidents that Mr. Goldenson was not in charge of, and all the vice-presidents, too. Not to mention the vice-presidents themselves, men in charge of so many things it gave me a charge just thinking about it.

Then into this room, one by one, come the little people — the people with the new show ideas. Each one in those days was given just ten minutes to present his case for his show. My presentation — I ask my readers, could it have been otherwise? — was masterful. I grabbed them with my opening teaser, held onto them for dear life through my characters and projected storylines, and closed with a stirring epilogue that literally throttled them.

When it was all over, I already knew the verdict. A pilot would indeed be made — and with just network money, too. Mr. Leonard Goldenson even spoke to me directly. "Mr. Amory," he asked, "are you going to write this show for us?"

Here, if you can believe it, I made a mistake. I said no — that I did not think any one person could write the show every week. I said that I thought that at the very least it would have to be me and another guy.

The simplicity of it was devastating. All of those executives became, in that one moment, in the face of such childlike honesty, children themselves. And, for the first time in network summit meeting annals, I believe, they all smiled. Let us do the worrying, they promised. *They* would get the "other guy."

Today, being an older and wiser man, I realize that what I should have said was yes, I would write the show. If I had said that, those executives would promptly have crowded $5,000 or so into my pockets every week under the "writing budget" and then I, like any other gracious writer-in-chief, would have gone out and hired somebody at, say, $1.25 an hour, given him a few hours each week to do a script, and then I would have taken home, by my figuring, $4,997.50.

Ah, the pity of it. But, no matter. After the meeting I went outside the room and held a celebration — not only with Mr. Cramer, but also with Mr. Cramer's then assistant, Mr. Leonard Goldberg. We drank a toast to the suc-

cess of "My Man St. John," and I of course made plans —
to go abroad, buy myself a TV station, and get a new
suit — all the things I had always wanted. Then very
quietly Mr. Goldberg spoke. "Cleve," he said, "I'm just a
poor boy from Brooklyn. But just between friends, what
the hell is a 'two-door companion'?"

That's the way he said it — "two-door companion" —
and I honestly think he thought it was some kind of automobile. He had been very busy, and he had not had
time to read the outline or the treatment. But it was really
touching. Here was a mere slip of a lad, but a network
executive nonetheless, who had fought the good fight for
the show — never failing, ever fighting — without even
knowing what it was he was fighting for. That man would
go far, I felt even then. And in truth he did. He went on,
in fact, from show to show and is still doing it, year after
year. As for the second "other guy" to write with me, it
was not a long wait for only a few days later Mr. Cramer
called me again. "What," he asked, "would you think of
the idea of Abe Burrows?"

Mr. Burrows! I exclaimed. Mr. Burrows! The famous
humorist and so-called Play Doctor of Broadway? The
man who would go to Philadelphia or New Haven when
a Broadway show was being tried out and in trouble and
after one evening seeing it would fix it right up for Broadway? Naturally, I told him I thought it was a wonderful
idea, but Mr. Cramer said, "Cleve, I want to warn you
about something. If Mr. Burrows does decide to do it, it
won't be quite all *your* show anymore."

He had emphasized the "your," but by now I had picked
up the lingo. Let me do the worrying, Doug boy, I told
him, you get Abe.

Meanwhile, just thinking of Abe Burrows as my other guy, I revised my plans. Never mind the trip abroad — I would go around the world. Never mind the TV station — I would buy *TV Guide*. And as for the new suit — well, I'd get the suit. I really needed it.

Mr. Burrows promptly wrote a first script using, I was glad to see, the same words I had used in my treatment of "My Man St. John," i.e., "He is not Hollywood's idea of a gentleman — he *is* a gentleman. He is a man who is very good at weekends, but not very good in the middle of the week." I was thrilled. And, not long after, Mr. Burrows himself called me. "Cleve," he said, "what do you think of the idea of Burl Ives to play Crackerby?" Mr. Ives! I exclaimed. Big Daddy himself! The great folksinger and humorist! I said I thought it was a wonderful idea. "But Cleve," Mr. Burrows continued, "I want to warn you about something. I don't know if we can get Ives, but even if we can it's going to mean giving up something. You see . . ." I cut him short. Let me do the worrying, Abe boy, I said, you get Burl.

To get Mr. Ives, however, it seemed we had to give up quite a bit — including, as it turned out, the show. For United Artists Television, who had Ives for a pilot about sailing the Caribbean, asked in return for their giving up Ives and their show, our show. Also Mr. Ives was not happy with the title of the show. He wanted the title of the show to be his. So in short order, "My Man St. John" became "O.K. Crackerby!" again.

Next came the fateful day when the pilot was actually being shot. I could hardly wait to get out to Hollywood to see it. I rushed to the Sam Goldwyn studios. The guard asked for my name. I gave it to him. He looked down a long list. "You're not on it," he said.

I smiled democratically. I know you have to be careful, I told him. I'm probably unlisted.

Finally when I did get in I learned the guard was not the only one who did not know I had anything to do with the show. Neither did anyone else. Eventually, though, I did get to meet somebody who introduced me to the executive producer, a man named Rod Amateau. He's a friend of Abe's, I was told. You see, it was explained to me, Abe won't actually be living with the show.

Mr. Amateau, it turned out, was evidently pretty busy, too. "O.K. Crackerby!" was just one of six shows he was apparently living with, including, I was sorry to learn, "My Mother, the Car." Nonetheless everyone was very excited about "O.K. Crackerby!" When it was tested by an audience rating system it tested the highest of all the year's new shows. No fewer than thirty-seven sponsors were lined up to sponsor it, and of the very first four to see it three bought it. To this day I often wonder what they saw.

But I put such thoughts behind me. The Number One New Show of the Season! Now even the trip around the world wasn't enough, not even *TV Guide*, not even my suit. Hang the expense — I'd get *two* suits.

I went to see the pilot in high spirits. With modest expectation I awaited my credit on the screen — that glorious line, "Created by Cleveland Amory." And there it was, all right — "Created by Abe Burrows and Cleveland Amory." Oh well, I thought magnanimously, Burrows did lend a hand, and anyway there would be other credits.

And sure enough there were — many of them, in fact. "Written by Abe Burrows," "Story Consultant, Abe Burrows," "Directed by Rod Amateau and Abe Burrows," and even "Theme by Rod Amateau and Abe Burrows."

Oh well, I thought, that's show business. And anyway, maybe now I was going to be so rich it would be imperative for me to remain anonymous. In any case, back in New York the new scripts began to roll in, by all sorts of writers. Evidently Mr. Burrows had gotten himself still another guy — and, in fact, another and another and another, as far as the eye could see. The only trouble was that, as these scripts rolled in and the shows appeared each week on the television, the one thing I could see was that any resemblance between them and the original idea of the show was purely coincidental.

The last one I remember before the show mercifully went off the air was evidently one of those scripts which Hollywood writers keep in their drawers — their desk drawers — to sell with appropriate name changes for any show. It told the story of a poor boy, the son of a man who owned a bake shop, who didn't seem to have any mother and who had therefore made up an animal, a griffin, to be his constant companion. The story also went on at some length into the story of the boy's schoolteacher and her relationship with his father.

At this point I left it, but at least for once in the "O.K. Crackerby!" experience I felt ahead of the game — they had written a show with an animal in it, even if it was a griffin.

If my first job had started poorly and had not, judging by "O.K. Crackerby!" on television, ended so hot either,

my first real job, postschool, was a different story. And I
had, at the Marathon Party, a friend whose family played
the crucial part in my getting the job in the first place. Her
name was Katharine Houghton, an actress and playwright, who was not only the niece of Katharine Hepburn,
but had played her daughter in "Guess Who's Coming to
Dinner," and was also the daughter of Ellsworth Grant,
my closest friend, next to Bruce, at college. Indeed, he
lived across from the Harvard house rooms Bruce and I
occupied. Ellsworth, a bright and charming fellow and,
like the Hepburns, from Hartford, had fallen in love with
Katharine Hepburn's second sister, Marian. Meanwhile,
in the course of meeting the rest of the Hartford Hepburn
clan, as fate or propinquity would have it, I fell in love
with the third sister, Peggy.

When Kathy Houghton arrived at the party I was still
involved with the Zinssers, so Marian had the job of in-
troducing Kathy around, and particularly to Polar Bear —
to whom she took an immediate shine and, most extraordinarily, one which was equally immediately returned.

It was really amazing. Polar Bear had met three brand-
new people at the party and he had batted three for three.
He liked them all. I took immediate credit for this extraordinary occurrence, of course. What else could it be
but the fact that I had chosen my guests so well.

Actually, in the case of Katharine, I really had no idea
how crazy about animals she had always been. Indeed, I
learned for the first time that she had had, as she put it,
"cats and dogs and rabbits and birds and God knows what
else, all of whom I liked more than people."

Polar Bear seemed to sense that Katharine was a real
animal person. Although there were already far too many

people for his taste in the apartment, and although the marathon was blaring over the television and the first runners were about to come by outside, despite all of this, all the noise and commotion inside and out, when Katharine went out on the balcony to watch the proceedings, to my amazement out on his balcony to watch beside her went Polar Bear. Even the helicopters flying overhead, over the runners, did not send him flying inside to his room and under the bed.

The arrival of Kathy Houghton, like Bill Zinsser, sent my mind back many years. I had spent almost every college weekend either in the winter in Hartford or in the summer at Fenwick, near Saybrook, where all good Hepburns repaired. And, fascinating as I found Katharine and her sisters, I found equally fascinating their father and mother. Dr. Hepburn was a particularly forceful person to whom I loved to address questions just to hear his invariably memorable answers. One day, during a period in which Katharine was receiving very poor personal notices around the country and was in fact regarded as "Box Office Poison," I was reading one of the two Hartford papers in which there was a story about Katharine returning from Hollywood for a visit to Hartford. The article was written in such glowing terms it might well have been a society page story about Hartford's most prominent debutante. I spoke of this to Dr. Hepburn and then gently mentioned the contrast with the press Katharine was receiving around the country. Dr. Hepburn lowered the part of the paper he was reading and fixed his formidable face on me. "Young man," he asked, "do you know what kind of work I do?" No, sir, I replied respectfully, I do not. "I thought not," Dr. Hepburn continued, "so I shall tell you.

I am a surgeon, and I specialize in what is politely known as the 'old man's operation.' " Oh, I said, but Dr. Hepburn was not yet through. "I have operated," he continued firmly, "on half of the newspaper publishers in this city, and I confidently expect, in good time, to operate on the other half. Does that," he asked, pushing up his paper again, "answer your question?"

It did indeed. Playing golf with Dr. Hepburn on Sunday morning was also a memorable experience. There were the usual Sunday morning social conflicts between those who wanted to play golf on Sunday morning and those who wanted everybody to go to church, but the fact that in the little resort of Fenwick the little church, called St. Mary's by the Sea, was right smack in the middle of the fairway of the fourth hole added a whole new dimension to conflicts elsewhere in society. Almost every Sunday the church was bombarded at least once and sometimes several times a day and indeed more than once in the summer a window was broken. Finally the idea took root among the churchgoers to pass a rule that, at the very least, and particularly on the fourth hole, all golf should cease between 11 A.M. and noon. This was naturally infuriating to the golfers, and this new controversy was in full height on a day when Dr. Hepburn was to play. Immediately he became part of a legendary story. In any case, that morning as luck, or rather bad luck, would have it Dr. Hepburn, teeing off on the fourth hole, hit a fine drive which bounced directly toward the church. Since it was a warm day the back doors were open, and the ball on its third or fourth bounce went directly into the church and up the aisle. As the congregation rose part in wrath and part in amusement, Dr. Hepburn without a word strode into the church, located his ball, put down his little canvas golf bag, selected his putter, and with a long firm stroke putted his way back out the way he had come in.

Mrs. Hepburn was an equally memorable character. An early founding member and leader of women's suffrage, she was a lifelong feminist in a day when being such was rare enough so that two young men as conservatively brought up as Ellsworth and myself found her both fascinating and at the same time sometimes as terrifying as her husband. Mrs. Hepburn was also, in contrast to her conservative husband, extremely radical in her views toward social issues and politics — to the point where an extraordinary number of dinner table arguments would end with some guest being so upset that Mrs. Hepburn would have to clap her hands and simultaneously announce the end of that discussion, and the beginning of a game.

I remember the day when I told Mrs. Hepburn that I was president of the *Harvard Crimson*. Immediately she asked me what I was going to do after college. You did not win many conversations with Mrs. Hepburn. Just the same, I liked to try to tease her, and I told her that once you had been president of the *Harvard Crimson* in your senior year at Harvard there was very little, in after life, for you.

Nonetheless, I believe it was her prodding that had much to do with the fact that I did take steps regarding my future employment. What I did was to go to Little, Brown and Company on Beacon Street. I could also have gone to Houghton Mifflin Company. They are both what we in Boston call perfectly good Boston institutions. In other words, they are a little bit better. I went directly to the head man — in Boston we do not trifle with middle-men — I told him he was indeed fortunate, and that I was one of the great writers of our time, and I had come to start my career at Little, Brown and Company. The man gave me a curious look. Did I realize, he asked, I would have to read other people's manuscripts? I told him I had not had much time to do much reading outside of my own writing, but I would try to help him. Then he gave me another curious look. Was I not afraid, he asked, that Little, Brown would kill my creative ambition? I told him I guessed that was just a chance I would have to take. Finally the man had had enough. Young man, he said, there is no job for you at Little, Brown and Company. This was a blow — right there in the heart of Beacon Hill. I must have looked very crestfallen because for the first time a rather pitying look came into his eyes, and he said, "You know, one of our editors just went down to Phila-delphia to join the staff of the *Saturday Evening Post*. They come out every week, you know. You could write every week for them."

I certainly was not going to take any haphazard sug-gestion from a man without the perspicacity to hire me. Nonetheless, I went home and decided to have a man-to-man discussion with my father. I brought up the sugges-tion about the *Saturday Evening Post*. My father considered the idea. Now, Philadelphia was not Boston — but then, what was? It was not New York — there was something to be said for it. Finally, I think what won him over was the fact that in those carefree, happy days the *Saturday Evening Post* printed on its cover "Founded A.D. 1728." It was the right century. Furthermore, after "Founded A.D. 1728" appeared the words "By Benj. Franklin." He was, after all, a Boston man even if he did take a rather extended trip to Philadelphia.

In short order I wrote a letter making an appointment to see the head man at the *Saturday Evening Post*. Before I heard from him, however, I went back to Mrs. Hepburn and told her of my experience with Little, Brown and Company. Mrs. Hepburn was very mad at Little, Brown and Company, but she was very excited about the *Saturday Evening Post*. "I have a friend there," she said, "Adelaide Neall. I'll write her about you."

I had forgotten all about this by the time I received a note from Wesley Winans Stout, editor of the *Saturday Evening Post*, in which he told me to come to the *Post* for an interview. When I arrived there I started out again that I was one of the great writers of our time — but Mr. Stout waved his hand. "Hm," he said, looking over my resume, "*Harvard Crimson*. You published a lot of humor, didn't you?" I could not make head or tail of this. Here was a man, the editor of the widest-read magazine in America, who simply did not know the difference between the *Harvard Crimson*, the undergraduate daily, and our hated mortal rival, the *Harvard Lampoon*, the undergraduate humor magazine. Obviously the man needed me. Actually, the *Harvard Crimson* had published very little humor — we took ourselves as seriously as it was possible to do and still survive in a changing world. But there was no time to quibble. "A lot of humor?" he asked again. I nodded vigorously. Enormous amount, I said. Just about every day.

In any case by the time the interview was over what I received was the job of Postscripts Editor. I was to be in charge of the short poem and prose pieces — the so-called

Postscripts — found on that particular page. I was also to be in charge of the cartoons on that page as well as the cartoons throughout the magazine.

For a young man just out of college to get such a job was almost incredible. All of the other editors — even if I was hardly then actually one of them — at the *Saturday Evening Post* had at least fifteen years' experience on a magazine or a newspaper. It was indeed so incredible that it was many weeks before I found out how it had happened. One thing was certain — it had practically nothing to do with either my resume, which in those days was rather longer than it is now, or my ridiculous line "one of the great writers of our time." What it did have to do with was three things. The first was that J. Bryan III, one of the editors and a distinguished man, had been doing postscripts for years and had become fed up with it, and that very morning before I arrived he had told the head editor as much. The second was, that as I mentioned, Mr. Stout had definitely confused the *Harvard Crimson* and the *Harvard Lampoon*, and thought at least he was getting a person with a lot of experience in humor. But the third and by far the most important reason was far more complicated. It concerned Mrs. Hepburn.

Mrs. Hepburn had indeed written her friend, Adelaide Neall, an editor at the *Saturday Evening Post* and a fellow Bryn Mawr alumna, about me. And though Adelaide Neall was an editor at the *Saturday Evening Post* her name as Adelaide W. Neall did not appear that way on the *Post* masthead. Although Ms. Neall was the only female editor at the *Post* in those days, it was felt that the appearance of even one female editor on the masthead might be disturbing to *Post* traditionalists and might even suggest a lessening of stature throughout the magazine. And so Ms. Neall's name invariably appeared, to the end of her life, as A. W. Neall.

When I thanked Mrs. Hepburn, and told her that story, her eyes flashed. "I knew they were conservative," she said, "but I never knew that." I knew what Mrs. Hepburn was thinking. I begged her not to write again, however, at least until I was firmly in harness. But I did want to know what she had said about me. "My letter was very short," she said. "I said, as I remember, 'Dear Adelaide, there is a man here who has taken a shine to Peg and the feeling seems to be reasonably reciprocal, and as for the rest of us, though we are not overboard on anybody his age, we are at least getting used to him. I understand he is going down to try to get a job at the *Saturday Evening Post*. I hope you help him. If you do not, I shall not allow your organ of privilege to enter this house again.' "

When Kathy Houghton came in from the balcony Polar Bear also came in. I thought about a story for which the Hepburns were responsible which involved considerable embarrassment for me. Actually, I had always felt Polar Bear enjoyed occasions when I was embarrassed. I think he did this because cats do not like to be embarrassed, and I had obviously been responsible for occasions which had been embarrassing for him.

In any case, the first of these stories concerned my being I believe as embarrassed as I ever remember being in New York. It came about at the time when I first came to New York and was actually for the first time being driven there in an automobile by none other than Katharine Hepburn herself. Just before she left me off where I was staying, at the Royalton Hotel, she asked me, since I was new to New York, if I knew many people. I told her not very many, whereupon she instructed me in a vague sort of way to call on her friend Tallulah Bankhead. "I'll call her about you," she said.

Of course I had not the slightest idea of taking her up on this. If there was a more formidable celebrity of that time in New York than Miss Hepburn it was certainly Miss Bankhead. Tallulah, as she was called by everybody, was a living legend not only for her talent and for her incredible voice but also for her temper as well as her temperament. All in all, she frightened even close friends, let alone total strangers.

Some days later, however, Katharine called me up and said I had not yet gone to see Tallulah. I was noncommittal. "You've got to do it," she said, "she's expecting you. Why don't you just drive up some Sunday lunchtime? Tallu loves people for Sunday lunch."

Now of course I had to go. Almost ill with nerves and worry I drove to Miss Bankhead's house in Bedford, New York, and arrived around one o'clock. The first piece of bad news was that there were dozens of cars parked in the driveway. The next was that even standing outside the door I could hear a bedlam of loud voices, raucous howls and gales of laughter. It took me literally minutes to get up the nerve even to press the bell. Even when I did I did it very timidly. Immediately, to my horror, the room full of voices I had just heard became absolutely silent. Finally the door opened, and the butler appeared. "Yes?" he said, somehow looking down on me although he was a full foot shorter. I am a friend of Katharine Hepburn's, I said earnestly. Miss Hepburn has, I believe, called Miss Bankhead about me.

The butler heaved a sigh as if he supposed that nowadays anything was possible and, after instructing me to wait, he left the door ajar and went back to the room. He obviously repeated what I had said because the next thing I heard was the unforgettably throaty sounds of Miss Bankhead's own voice. "Tell him," she shouted, "I'll be damned if I can see every damned one of Kate Hepburn's goddamned friends." At this there were roars of laughter which kept up all the time the butler was returning to me. "I'm sorry," he said, "but Miss Bankhead seems to be busy right now. Perhaps some other time."

I could scarcely believe my good fortune — I could get away. Immediately and gratefully I turned around to flee, but before the butler could shut the door there was one more terror in store for me. Once more Miss Bankhead's voice roared from the room. "Is he," she asked, "handsome?" I tried to move on out, but the butler caught up with me and once more took a survey. "Well," shouted Miss Bankhead, "what the hell are you doing? I asked you if he was handsome!"

At this I must have turned so bright red that even the butler was sorry for me, because as he moved away and back toward the room he said, rather pityingly, "Passably." I must have passed muster because this time he took me back inside.

Still beet red, I was marched around and introduced by Miss Bankhead herself. I never did enjoy that first visit very much, but in no time at all I either outgrew it or forgot it because Miss Bankhead and I became, if not fast friends — a dangerous phrase to use with her — at least good friends. Indeed, from that time on I had many memorable Sunday lunches with Miss Bankhead, as well as trips to the Polo Grounds to see her beloved New York Giants.

Also, although I did not marry Peggy Hepburn, I did through the years stay friends with the whole Hepburn family. My most recent meeting with Katharine was when her book, *Me*, came out. I went over to congratulate her on it, and in talking, as we often do, around each other rather than at each other — because there are usually so many others present — I asked her if it was not terribly sad for her that Peg had for some incredible reason chosen to marry a Bennington professor instead of me. Did she not realize, I teased, what her sister had given up? And if she could not realize it, why could she not think of Peg, and realize the wonderful life she could, as my wife, have had? Did she not ever think about it? "Not ever," Katharine replied, "and neither does Peg." Why, I demanded. "Because," Katharine said firmly, "you have no chacter." She made, in the New England way, only two syllables out of the word. I told her sternly I knew I was somewhat deficient in character, but I did not appreciate having one of the most prominent women in the world going around blabbing the fact. I paused meaningfully. And furthermore, I continued, I demanded to know there and then what evidence she had for her slanderous charge.

In response Ms. Hepburn asked me, for the record and in front of all those people, if by any chance I remembered one time late in the summer when Howard Hughes was visiting, and she and Howard were playing tennis every morning with Peg and me and golf every afternoon, how in between times Peg would often make me take a swim. And how, she added, on one particular occasion, when Mr. Hughes and she happened to be watching from the house with binoculars, they clearly saw Peg dive in and swim some fifty yards or so, and at the same time they also saw me do nothing but duck under the pier and then jump up and rub a towel around myself. I was clearly demonstrating, for their benefit, how invigorating it was. And, since I did not on that occasion so much as get a toe wet, I had no character.

It was my turn to take the stand. In the first place, I said, by spying on us and using binoculars, they were nothing but Peeping Toms and should not be believed. In the second place, Connecticut water in October was below freezing, and nobody but a damned Hepburn would even consider going in it.

Although I had received the job of Postscripts Editor, I still had not achieved my ambition — which was to write for the *Saturday Evening Post*. In many ways, how this came about was as memorable, at least to me, as was how I got the Postscripts Editor job.

The way it happened was that I had worked at the magazine no more than three days when a memorandum came down from the head editor, Mr. Stout, to all the editors. Somehow it had been put on my desk, too. "What would you think," the editor asked in this memorandum, "of an article on Groton School?" All the editors had written in large letters beside their initials, "NO." Now my initials were not on the memorandum. The secretarial work there had been slipshod. As a matter of fact, one of my jobs was to take the memoranda from my desk at one end of the editorial line back to Mr. Stout's desk at the other end of the line. They did not have an office boy. Nonetheless, I seized the memorandum and wrote in large letters "YES," and beside this I wrote my initials. I then took the memorandum back. I had hardly returned to my desk when my buzzer sounded and Mr. Stout announced that he wished to see me. This time I was barely inside his door when he swung around in a great swivel chair. "Why," he said, "did you put yes on my suggestion for an article on Groton?" He pronounced it Growton. Groton, I corrected him, pronouncing it Grotten. He was obviously a man of limited range. He ignored, however, my correction. "I understand," he said, "there is a remarkable man up there named Dr. Peabody." He pronounced this Pea-body. Once again I corrected him. The name Peabody, I told him slowly, because it would obviously take him time to take it all in, is pronounced in Boston by saying the consonants as rapidly as possible and ignoring all vowels. It's Pbd, Pbd, I said, doing it a second time so that he would get the hang of it.

I then explained to him that Dr. Peabody had built Groton School on the British idea of the American idea of the British public or American private school. I also told him that Dr. Peabody was indeed, as he said, a remarkable man and that he was, though a man in his eighties, still exercising on the Groton campus at recess every morning — with dumbbells. The push-up kind, I quickly added, of course.

I also firmly emphasized how strict Groton was. I told him the story of a young Groton boy, who on being told he would have to see Dr. Peabody at the conclusion of the school day, was manfully being consoled by a classmate. Maybe, he said, it's just a death in the family.

In any case, after I had finished telling Mr. Stout about Groton School, he thought a moment and then spoke. "You know," he said, "I think we will have an article on —" he paused "— that school." This, I realized, was my opportunity. Mr. Stout, I said, I would like to have a chance to do the text of that article. Once more he thought a moment, and then looked up again. "You know," he said, "it might be a rather amusing thing to send a Groton boy back on that article."

This I could not let pass. Mr. Stout, I said, I did not go to Groton. I went to Milton Academy. What I told you about Groton School was common knowledge. Milton Academy was founded in 1797 — we regard Groton as a rather new school. I started telling Mr. Stout all about Milton Academy, but he held up his hand. I had already found, dealing with people outside Boston, that they cannot take too much at any one time. Regular doses, regularly repeated, at regular intervals was far better — otherwise they could become ill.

Even if I did not get to tell Mr. Stout about Milton Academy I did get the chance to do the article on Groton, and the article came out, too — with my name on it, and with color pictures.

It was my very first published work, a landmark in my life. And not a one of you out there remember it, do you? It is just one of the many crosses I have had to bear.

The reason was simple. They had, at the *Saturday Evening Post*, a man whom they called Title Editor. He was the man responsible for putting the titles on the articles after the writers were finished with them. Remember, I had not been there long. It was a large staff, and I had not been able to educate them all. That man would have taken time — he was a man from New Jersey.

In any case the Groton article, my first published work, a landmark, as I say, in my life, appeared in the *Saturday Evening Post* under the title "Goodbye, Mr. Peebs."

After the Groton article I moved to Arizona — the northern part, of course. My father always said that nothing good ever came out of a warm climate.

CHAPTER FOUR

My Last Duchess and 4,000 Other Celebrities

There were many times in my early writing career in which I believe Polar Bear, who had not then of course been born, could have been most useful — if for no other reason than to keep me from getting involved in undertakings which would have far better not been undertaken by anyone at all, even including an undertaker. I do not mean by this that Polar Bear could not always have made me cease and desist from some project which from the beginning held little prospect of success or, from his point of view, was not part of a joint operation which involved, whether successful or not, at least togetherness.

But, given plenty of time, he could, make no mistake, have done so. Indeed, in his devious little way, he could very rapidly concoct some plan which would make what I had wanted to do, and what he did not want me to do, impossible.

In such endeavors not only did he not play by the rules, he was also manifestly unfair. If, for one example, what I wanted to do involved leaving him for some time — which he could tell from suitcases, tickets, etc. — he would immediately feign a desperate and obviously life-threatening illness — one from which, the moment I had cancelled all plans, he could equally immediately feign a complete and miraculous recovery. If, for another example, I had undertaken something which he thought might involve an intimate association with someone who to him was an unseemly and entirely inappropriate other human — such as someone coming for what seemed to him an interminably long visit — he would not even bother with feigning illness, he would simply disappear. At this, it goes without saying, I would immediately be sure he had somehow gotten out the door and I would not only have the job of looking for him outside the apartment, I would also have the job of looking for him inside. And it was amazing how many places to hide he could find in a small apartment. When I eventually did find him in one of those hiding places in the apartment — he never went outside — he would have made his point and, as far as he was concerned, the longer it took the better.

Why then did I undertake a project — be it anything

from a change of career to a human visitor of which he so disapproved? I can only plead that writing is lonely work — and it was particularly so for me in the days before Polar Bear. It was also particularly then not much, if indeed any, fun. The best you can say for writing is that, in retrospect, it can be some fun when someone who has read something you have written has something nice to say about it. But even in this case, remember it doesn't come until later, and even then you still remember the pain of what you went through to begin with before there was any fun. Altogether, I believe Dr. Johnson put it best. "Nobody," he said, "but a blockhead ever wrote except for money" — to which I have always thought he should have added, "or to meet a deadline." I have also thought, however, that there is something about that word "deadline" that to me symbolizes the whole trouble with writing.

Not to put too fine a point, as the English say, upon my point, since writing is the way it is, when you are a writer almost anything except writing seems a far more interesting thing to be doing. Cleaning up the house, sharpening pencils, telephoning, rearranging books, even reading something you have read quite recently — these all seem infinitely superior occupations compared with the job of actually putting your own words on paper. And when someone promises you some excitement — a luncheon, even with someone you do not care that much about, a visit with someone who, for the life of you, you cannot remember where or when you met, or even another job which, although it may demand some writing, at least offers besides the writing a new and possibly amusing change of scenery and people — the chances are a writer will fall for such an opportunity every time. Certainly in one particular example of this I fell for it hook, line and sinker — something which, in another era with Polar Bear on guard, would never have happened.

It all began in the form of a hand-delivered letter to my apartment from the New York Waldorf-Astoria Towers with a large "E" on the front of the envelope. In those days, if you received a hand-delivered letter from the New York Waldorf-Astoria Towers with a large "E" on the envelope, you were some pumpkins. You had gone about as far socially — up or perhaps down, depending on how you looked on it — as it was possible to go.

This was because, not to beat about the bush, what you had done was to receive a letter from no less a personage than His Royal Highness, the Duke of Windsor. In those days there may have been higher mucky-mucks socially, at least in one particular echelon of our Society, than the Duke and Duchess of Windsor, but there were not many and they did not last as long.

Although I had met the Duke and Duchess socially on several occasions, I should say that I did not receive the letter for this reason. What had brought me to their attention was a few paragraphs I had written about them staying at White Sulphur Springs in a book I called *The Last Resorts*. In any case, in the first part of his letter the Duke of Windsor called attention to what I had written about them, and in the second part he went on to invite me to the Waldorf-Astoria Towers for tea.

Of course the fact that the invitation was to tea took some of the social bloom off the rose. I was brought up in Boston by parents who were uncommonly strict about which meals to which it was proper to invite strangers, and which it was not. Dinner, for example, was out of the question — you did not know the people. Luncheon? Possibly, but luncheon could be tricky, too. Cocktails? Certainly not. Cocktails in the Boston of my day had never arrived at the kind of mass media they are today. Assuming people rarely invite anyone to breakfast, except for dubious reasons, that left only tea. Tea was the most democratic of all Boston institutions. You could ask almost anyone to tea — within reason, of course.

In any case, the die had been cast. It was tea to which the Duke of Windsor had invited me, and although I could have, had I wished, taken umbrage that it was not to be luncheon or dinner, tea is what it would be. If nothing else, I reasoned — always favorable to myself of course — after our meeting the Duke would no longer have such a gap in his social knowledge of Boston.

For better or worse, I accepted. And, when I arrived at the Royal Suite of the Waldorf-Astoria Towers at the appointed five o'clock hour, I found not only the Duke of Windsor but also the Duchess of Windsor and three Pug dogs. At this point I should say that I had, before this time, very little acquaintance with Pug dogs except at a distance. And, now that I think of it even today, I do not believe Polar Bear had ever met a Pug in his entire life. Indeed, as a matter of fact I am willing to bet that if he did, he kept it at a distance.

Nonetheless, I was then, and am still, partial to all kinds of animals, even ones I have not met, and I certainly had no wish, particularly early in my relationship with the Windsors, to take either the pro-Pug or anti-Pug side. I know very well there are people who like Pugs and that, conversely, there are Pugs who like people. I also have a theory and that is that people who like a certain kind of dog and have them all their life often grow, in later life, to look more and more like them — or else the kind of dog they like grows to look more and more like them, I am really not quite sure which. Originally I knew the Duke liked Cairn Terriers, and certainly if there was one animal he seemed to me to resemble it was a Cairn Terrier. On the other hand the Duchess liked Pugs, and there was something about the way she did her hair — parted in the middle — or indeed the whole shape of her face, particularly the jaw, that made her seem to resemble a Pug.

One thing I noticed at that very first meeting was that Pugs liked to sleep a lot. They were asleep when I got there, and they were asleep when I left. After I got to know the Windsors better I grew to understand this and I did not blame them. It was, however, a little disconcerting at first. It was also disconcerting in that there were three Pugs, and they all snored — and not in concert, either.

The Duke of Windsor began the conversation by saying that he had written his book and now it was, as he put it, "the Duchess' turn." But the Duchess would need, as he also put it, "some assistance" — to which he added they were looking for someone with humor since she was known to be so witty.

I believe at that even Polar Bear would have smelled a mouse — but for some reason I did not. The only excuse I have is that there was something about being with the Windsors that seemed to make people not think about what they had just heard — either because of the way the Windsors said it or because of the whole strange aura of royalty in which it occurred. As Henry Adams once said about his father, Charles Francis Adams, who was Ambassador to the Court of St. James', "He was one of the exceedingly small number of Americans who were indifferent to Dukes and Duchesses and to whom Queen Victoria was nothing more than a slightly inconvenient person."

I knew I could hardly measure up to Charles Francis Adams' standard, particularly since at this stage I had no idea what kind of assistance the Windsors were looking for. But at least I did not hesitate to explain that I had never been a ghost writer before and I did not particularly like the idea. I did add, though, that if the Duchess' book was to be an autobiography as told to me, that might be a different story.

The Duchess said nothing, which was an ominous sign, but the Duke seemed to indicate that would be all right. My only other question was to ask them if they had any idea what the book might be called. I still had in my mind that experience about "Goodbye Mr. Peebs" and I did not intend to go through that again. Just as I was thinking about this, the Duke said that so far for the Duchess' book they had not come up with a title. Did I have any suggestions? I told him I did not but that I would think about it, and would at least be happy to make a suggestion.

On that note we said goodbye — with the Pugs not only still sleeping but also not giving me the benefit of so much as a parting snore. In between that visit and the next, however, I spent a good deal of time thinking of a possible title for the Duchess of Windsor's memoirs as told to me, and one idea seemed promising — something to do with the controversy over the Duchess not having been given the title Her Royal Highness, which she craved — but instead being given merely the title Her Grace. Both she and the Duke were so upset about this that, though it happened early on after the Duke's abdication, they spent most of the rest of their lives complaining about it.

I had thought a good deal about this, and on my next visit to the Windsors I told them I thought I had a suggestion for a title for the Duchess' book. Both the Duke and the Duchess were very pleased about this, and I think even the Pugs would have been, too, but the butler had taken them out for a walk before they could hear it. The Duke was in fact so pleased that he could hardly wait to hear my suggestion. "What is it?" he asked, "what is it?"

Untitled, I said.

There was a dead silence. I was not surprised. I had already learned that the Windsors were in a very difficult position where humor was concerned. If no one laughed at something or no one told them something somebody said was a joke they would not venture so much as a smile — obviously for fear it was not a joke. In this case, although I hoped my title was humorous, it was not just a joke. Rather it was, I thought, an effective way to ward off, at the very beginning of her book, the criticism of the Duchess being so angry about not getting the title Her Royal Highness — and that, indeed, rather than being angry about it, she thought it was amusing.

Finally, though, the silence was over. "I think, Amory," the Duke said thoughtfully, "we'll have to get some more opinions on this thing."

One thing was certain. Between then and my next visit the Windsors obviously did not just go ask anybody for an opinion on my title — instead they went, at least from their point of view, to the very top opinionated people they knew. First of all, they asked the Duke's own solicitor, Sir George Allen. Next they asked none other than the British press czar, Lord Beaverbrook, whose paper had already contracted for the Duchess' memoirs. And, finally they even asked, as a kind of outside opinion, Lord Astor. But that was okay at that time — the thing that happened to Lord Astor later had not yet happened.

When I arrived to hear about the verdict on my title I knew right away that the news was not good. I had already learned in the time I had been with the Windsors that if there was good news you got it from the Duchess — if there was bad news you got it from the Duke. They had, it seemed, their marriage all worked out. And this time, because the Duchess was not even there — and neither for that matter were the Pugs — there was just the Duke, so I was certain it was bad news.

The Duke was very nice about it. "The trouble, Amory," he said, stammering slightly, "is that the H.R.H., H-her R-royal H-highness, which the D-duchess did not r-receive, is not a t-title, it's an ap-appellation." He paused. "Could you do anything with the word ap-appellation?" It was my turn for a long silence. I did think of *Unappellated*, but frankly the more I thought about it the more I was sure it would not fly.

Still not knowing what my masterpiece — or perhaps I should say *our* masterpiece — was to be called, I left for Paris to meet the Windsors in the early spring. I sailed on the *Queen Mary* and had a delightful crossing, since my tablemates in the Queen's Grill included the famous playwright George S. Kaufman and the consummate humorist actor Clifton Webb. Arriving in Paris, I stayed at the Traveller's Club until I could choose a hotel. I was extremely careful in my selection of this and finally, from a position across the way, chose not only the hotel I wanted, the Hotel Normandy, near the Louvre, but also the very room. I wanted one which I could see from my vantage point had a balcony halfway around the hotel. Even today when I think of the room I realize that this balcony, properly wired of course so that he could not have fallen off, would have been perfect for Polar Bear. In any case, keeping in mind exactly what floor the room was on, I marched into the lobby of the Normandy, found the concierge, and instructed him to follow me — my mind still firmly on the exact room. Getting off at the ninth floor, I took the concierge directly to the door and addressed him in my best Milton Academy French. *Voilà*, I said, putting my finger firmly on the door, *ma chambre*. But the concierge refused to open the door. *"C'est occupé,"* he said. I told him, in that case, to unoccupé it immediately. *"Ah, monsieur,"* he sighed, *"c'est impossible."*

Finally we struck a deal. As soon as the place was unoccupied he was to call me immediately. And, to his credit he did. I moved in on that very day and in short order put to work not only the concierge but also two bellmen and a maid. I really made an incredible number of changes — a standup desk, really a painter's easel, which I had put next to an opened window looking out on the balcony, a king-sized bed instead of the pipsqueak-sized creation they had there, a large stuffed chair, and no wire wastebaskets but real, masterful wastebaskets ready to take a wide variety of mistakes.

At last everything was to my satisfaction, and late that

afternoon all five of us — myself, the concierge, the maid, and the bellmen, sat down in total exhaustion. Once more I turned to my Milton Academy French to break the last impasse. *Ma chambre est parfait,* I said. *Mais il y a encore un peu de difficulté.* "*Ah non, monsieur,*" the concierge protested, in a voice as exhausted as he was. "*Ce n'est pas possible. Qu'est ce que sait?*" I looked at him sternly. *Qu'est ce que sait est très simple, monsieur,* I replied. *La chambre est un peu trop chère.* The concierge looked stricken. Needless to say, however, after all the rearranging, all the furniture moving, all the new furniture, not to mention the fact that I had mentioned I would be staying there at least until fall, he could do nothing but lower the price — the first and only time I have ever succeeded in accomplishing such a thing in a French hotel. And indeed, once that was settled everything was truly perfect. It was really a wonderful room with a terrific balcony and I looked forward to a delightful spring, summer, and fall.

There was, however, one large fly in the ointment — and that was the job itself. My disillusionment was not long in coming. It happened over a tape recorder which the publishers had sent over for the Duchess to use in dictating to me. In one of my very first sessions with her she said something about her childhood, then in the very next session I had with her she said something that was totally different about exactly the same event. I asked her about this, explaining that I had played both sections back on the recorder to confirm the difference. At this the Duchess became very irritated. "They told me," she said, "that that tape recorder was not for me, it was for you, and I want you to remember that."

One thing I could not fail to notice was that whatever the Duke had given up by his abdication he certainly did not give up his standard of living. The Windsors had two houses and a total of thirty servants — all to look after just two people. Their main residence was a château in the Bois du Boulogne which had formerly been the home of Charles de Gaulle. On the outside the house was formidable enough — complete with a large park, two garages, two greenhouses, a gatekeeper's lodge, and a long driveway including a high black lamppost topped by a gilded crown. But from the inside it was truly breathtaking. One entered a marble hall, on one side of which was a huge sedan chair and on the right an even more huge globe of the Earth. Next to strike a visitor's eye was a huge carving flanked by sconces and swags of the Royal Arms. As if this were not enough, up the marble stairway, from a thick staff, hung the banner of the Knights of the Garter. Moving on to the drawing room, there were two full-length portraits, one of Queen Mary and the other of the Duke as Prince of Wales in his Garter robes. In the east end of this room, which opened onto the dining room, was an enormous portrait of the Duchess, square-faced and square-jawed, of which perhaps the kindest thing was said by Sir Cecil Beaton. "It looks," he said, "nothing like her." In actuality, most people found the portrait looked exactly like her.

Finally, upstairs one came to the Duchess' suite and the Duke's, the Duchess' being distinguished by a huge heap of cushions, each one embroidered with mottoes which included one entitled "My Romance," and another "British Reserve." I also noticed that the only photograph on the Duchess' bedside table was, of all people, Queen Mary. As for the Duke's suite, it was small and Spartan, the only similarity with the Duchess' being a few of the same mottoed cushions. Of these my favorite was the curious one "A Night In Cherbourg." There were also, I was told, two guestrooms and a bath on the top floor, but these were apparently rarely used. The Duchess' excuse for not inviting friends to stay was simple. "There are not," she would say, "enough guest bathrooms."

The Windsors' second home was Le Moulin de la Tuilerie, an old mill on twenty-five acres near the little village of Gif-sur-Yvette in Seine-et-Oise. Bought for $80,000 from Étienne Drian, a fashion artist and stage designer, it was transformed by the Windsors and some million dollars into an English country house. Here the Duke, who loved the house, had a small room with hardly more than an army cot for a bed, while the Duchess, who never liked the house or for that matter living in the country, had a huge bedroom which was all white except for large beams overhead. These were waxed and gilded, and stood over a truly vast four-poster bed.

Actually the mill consisted of four buildings, the main one of which backed up to a millstream and a picturesque waterfall. Inside, while nearly everything seemed to be colored a bright red, which gave the whole house an overly rich-looking motif, it was also dominated by seemingly endless chintz. In one part of the mill, which was the former barn, the Duke had all his personal trophies and souvenirs. In front of the fireplace in this room the Duchess pointed out, especially for my benefit it seemed to me, a funny twisted red stool — one which, she said, the Duke used to like to sit on and rest while elephant hunting in East Africa. She could, I am sure, imagine what appeal this had for me.

The Windsor "day" would begin at ten-thirty, when the Duchess' maid would wake her for breakfast and bring her the newspapers. In most social set-ups of Windsor proportions the mistress of the house would begin her after-breakfast day by giving "the order of performances" first to the butler, then to the head chef, third to the head gardener, and fourth and finally to the head chauffeur. For the Windsors, however, the first to be summoned would be the Duke. This occurred at exactly eleven-thirty, at which time he would literally be given his marching orders for the day. These were almost invariably menial — to tell the first chauffeur to take the chef to market, to tell the second chauffeur about something she wanted him to pick up, or to tell the head gardener something she wished him to look after before he came to see her.

By one o'clock the Windsors' custom-built royal blue Cadillac would be at the front door ready to take the Duchess to lunch either at a friend's house or at a restaurant, then to take her in the afternoon either to a bridge game or one of her daily appointments with a hairdresser, masseuse, chiropodist, or perhaps to view a dress collection at Chanel, Dior, Mainbocher, Balmain, or Givenchy — after which the car would pick her up to be back in time to instruct the servants on how to arrange and place the flowers for the evening. She required at least three hours to prepare herself for dinner.

Meanwhile, of course, the Duke would be either playing golf or, if he had no golf game, gardening. On one day when it was raining, and he could not play golf, he took me to Versailles and gave me a personal tour. For me it was an extremely memorable day because he made interesting comments on just about all the kings — it was one subject which he knew extremely well.

The remarkable thing was that very rarely did the Duke see the Duchess from their eleven-thirty appointment in the morning until the guests arrived — which they did almost every night, unless the Windsors were going out — in the evening. When these guests did arrive, particularly for a formal Bois house dinner, that scene, too, was memorable to me. From the entrance hall, fragrant with incense and dark — it was lit by candelabra only — the guests hardly knew where to go, but in time a butler would escort them to the drawing room where he would bring everybody to "sign in," as it were, in the handsome guest book.

Finally, ushered into the drawing room, the guests would find footmen in full scarlet livery ready to offer them a wide variety of drinks — from cocktails to champagne. These drinks, however, were only offered twice — for good reason. As the Duchess well knew, if the Duke had more than that there would be trouble — he had, to put it gently, an extremely light head. Indeed, the Duchess never allowed the cocktail hour to last more than forty-five minutes and often not until after it did she appear — at the head of the stairs to march down very much like royalty. Most of the guests, I noticed, curtseyed not only to the Duke but also to the Duchess — although, without the Royal Highness appellation, she was not entitled to this. The butler's announcement of dinner was equally pointed. He ignored the Duke altogether and then, bowing low to the Duchess, said in a voice clearly audible to everybody, "Your Royal Highness, dinner is served."

The Duchess did not believe in more than ten at a table.

If there were more than that there were two tables, with the Duchess presiding at one and the Duke at another. The food was truly outstanding, as might be expected from the fact that the Duchess had a chef who had formerly been the chef of the Aga Khan and was rated as one of the best in the world. Again, whatever the Duke had given up by abdicating he did not give up in the gastronomic field — with, that is, the exception of soup. The Duchess could not stand soup. "An interesting liquid," she liked to say, "which gets one nowhere." Nonetheless, other than soup I have never had food at a private house to match what was served at the Windsors'. On one occasion, when I had lunch with the Duchess, just the two of us, no less than nine courses were served. Of these, the Duchess did hardly more than taste each course — somehow, it seemed to me, as if to prove her classic statement, "A woman can never be too rich or too thin."

Speaking of rich, the Windsors were indeed so. The Duke received from the British government over a million pounds a year tax free. He also had a large account at the Morgan Bank in New York which, acting on stock tips from his rich friends including the Dillons, the Mellons, the Biddles, the Paleys, and the Robert Youngs, he had managed to raise to several million dollars. As for the Duchess, the jewels alone which the Duke had given her — many from his family's collection, which were of course not his to give — were worth many millions, and when they were sold at auction after her death went, along with her other effects, for $50 million.

Despite this, the Windsors promoted the idea among their friends that the wolf was almost always at their door. There were countless stories that when they went to visit for a weekend or even to attend a single dinner party they were paid for doing so. This was not true, but the fact is they had an angle on almost everything to do with money. If, for example, a friend said he wanted to give them a present, the Duchess would immediately say, "Don't send anything here — send it in care of the British Embassy. Otherwise we'll have to pay duty." Even the Windsor automobiles were bargains. The royal blue Cadillac, for example, built to the Duke's specifications, was a gift from the Chairman of the Board of General Motors — so was the Buick station wagon with the Royal Crest on it — and both were sent care of the British Embassy. The main house was owned by the City of Paris but was leased to the Windsors for the incredible sum of fifty dollars a year. The French government forgave them all income taxes and, in the end, all death duties. On top of it all, the Duke was reputed to be the largest dealer in French francs on the black market.

Just the same, I never heard either the Duke or the Duchess say one good word about the French. When the Windsors went out late at night to a French nightclub, the Duke delighted in asking for a German song, and at the times when I ate alone with them at a French restaurant I was not only embarrassed about how they would go on with their talk about the French, I was actually concerned that the waiters might have slipped something, if not in the soup, then in some other dish.

The Windsor dinner parties attracted very few French or even English notables, but they did attract a wide variety of all kinds of Americans. The head of the American armed forces — or indeed all Allied forces — was, for example, in regular attendance. So were what seemed to me a rather motley group of American celebrities. The Duchess indeed kept up on all the arrivals of celebrities in Paris by her subscription to *Celebrity Service,* and rarely failed to see that one she wanted received an invitation to dinner. When a prominent American author would arrive in Paris, the Duchess would not only send an invitation but instruct me to get one of his or her books. When I did this, she would ask me to pick out a particularly good line, and then during the dinner when there was total silence she would turn to the author and say, "I really think your line" — and then she would slowly quote the exact line — "is so wonderfully put." After she had done this, at least one guest would always say to a companion, "Isn't that just like the Duchess? She keeps up on everything." On top of something, mind you, that even Polar Bear, in his sleep, could have seen through.

If the dinners were interesting so were the luncheons, particularly those in the spring and summer at the mill. My all-time favorite was a luncheon at which the celebrity guest was none other than Dorothy Kilgallen, then one of the panelists on the famous TV game show, "What's My Line?" The idea of this show was to have the celebrity panelists try to guess the occupation of the non-celebrity guest.

That Saturday morning I was picked up in the Windsors' blue Cadillac — which attracted, as it was obviously supposed to, a large degree of attention. I climbed into the front seat and had hardly settled in when I saw that in the back seat were Ms. Kilgallen and her husband. To say they were not pleased to see me was an understatement. They clearly believed they were on their way to some engagement far grander than one which would be attended by me. And while they were not adverse to having me not-so-subtly clearly understand this, I, in turn, could not resist indicating to them that I went to the Windsors' almost every day.

Nonetheless, when we arrived at our destination and went into lunch, Ms. Kilgallen's spirits were revived when she found herself seated at the Duke's right. She was particularly pleased when she saw that not only was I not on the Duchess' right, but that seated there was none other than the commanding chief of the American forces in Europe. In any case, lunch proceeded in fine form outdoors on the mill grounds until, just after dessert, the Duchess suddenly clapped her hands and asked if anyone could guess what we were all going to do next. No one could. "We are going," said the Duchess with an excited smile, "to play 'What's My Line?' " With that, immediately the waiters whisked away the luncheon dishes, while the footmen set one long table in front of the luncheon tables, and moved the guests' chairs into an audience-like position. While this was going on, as quietly as possible I asked the Duchess how she proposed to play the game. "You'll see," the Duchess said sharply. "Don't be a spoilsport. You're always so negative." The Duchess then turned to the whole audience. "Now," she said, clapping her hands again, "Dorothy and I are going to be two of the panelists, and the General and —" she looked around, I thought a little bit desperately "— Mr. Amory will be the other two."

As we took our seats behind the long table, the Duke, who was sitting in the front row of the audience, suddenly held up his hand. "Can I," he asked, "be the first guest?" How can we guess him, in a low voice I asked the General, seated beside me, he doesn't do anything. I did not, however, keep my voice low enough, for the Duchess, who had obviously been considering the Duke's request, suddenly clapped her hands again. "No, you can't be the first guest," she said, "everybody knows you don't do anything." At this, of course, all the guests burst out laughing. The Duke looked at first very disappointed, then suddenly he brightened. "I know what," he said, "I'll make up being somebody else." Everybody apparently thought this was a terrific idea, and the game was about to begin, when suddenly the Duke spoke again. "I've got it," he said, "I'll be an airline pilot."

There, of course, went game No. 1. Eventually the audience gave up on the Duke as a guest, but a long succession of other people, one after another, attempted to make up being somebody. I have played a lot of games at a lot of parties in my life — in fact I once did a whole article entitled "The Gamey Crowd" — but I do not think that ever in my life, at any house or house party, have I ever seen such determination to keep a really terrible idea going. The worst thing was that nobody could stop until the honored guest — in this case not Ms. Kilgallen but the General — got up to leave. When he finally did the entire audience and panel too, as I recall, burst into loud applause. Actually, it was the only applause "What's My Line?" received all afternoon.

Early on I realized that one of the many problems I faced in the book was how to get rid of the Duchess' previous two husbands prior to the Duke. Both of these were still living at the time I took on the job, and they were of course the real stumbling block to her becoming

Queen of England. An extraordinary number of Americans believed the British would not accept her because she was an American. This, however, was not true. The British would have accepted an American, but they found one with two living ex-husbands, as they would put it, a very sticky wicket.

I suggested to the Duchess that what we should do with these ex-husbands was to assign them faults — faults so terrible that the reader would not only understand why she eventually had to divorce them, but would also understand how, in contrast to them, the Duke who, though he had a fair share of faults of his own, would somehow be believable as the true love of her life. Not just, in other words, because he was a king but because he was such a terrific person.

The Duchess basically liked the idea and, since she had none of her own, we decided to go ahead with it. Her first husband was Lieutenant (j.g.) Earl Winfield Spencer, whom she had met in Pensacola when she had gone to visit her cousin. "Every generation," she told me, "has its own set of heroes, and mine were flyers." Nonetheless, among the many faults we assigned to this hero were selfishness, bossiness, and demandingness, and we also zeroed in on the major fault we assigned him, which was drinking. Indeed, with the Duchess' prodding I soon had Lieutenant (j.g.) Earl Winfield Spencer having a snort on almost every page. When, however, the Duchess was still not satisfied with this but wanted to keep adding to it, I had to protest. I reminded her that if we did not let up a bit we would not be able to stop the reader from wanting to join him.

But even the problem of how much Lieutenant Spencer

should be drinking was as nothing compared to the problem of his job — which, after their marriage, was teaching naval air cadets to fly, first at Pensacola in Florida, and later at the Coronado Air Force base in California. Having that job in those days of extremely primitive planes — and on top of it, being a heavy drinker — was hardly a believable situation. And, if this was not difficult enough, I still faced another problem attendant on it. This was, very simply, the date when all of it was occurring. The Duchess had made very clear to me at our very first meeting that she did not want any dates in the book, but she soon added another injunction — that she did not want any well-known events in the book which the readers could very easily date for themselves.

That left us with such a large problem that it made the others seem modest by comparison. Here we had Lieutenant (j.g.) Earl Winfield Spencer flying around and drinking and at the same time trying to teach young naval air cadets to fly — all in preparation for a war we couldn't mention. Presumably, if it had been World War II it would have worked like a charm. But the fact was, it wasn't — it was World War I.

On one occasion I did manage to pry out of the Duchess a sort of postscript about the final difference she had with Lieutenant Spencer. She expressed it to me as follows:

One of the things that made my personal life so difficult was that Win did not have my facility for getting to know people. He also did not have the slightest ability at divining people's motives. I most certainly did — in fact, it was at this period in my life that I realized for the first time that I had a real and truly extraordinary gift for being able to see through people. It irritated me almost beyond endurance that Win could not understand this. I used to warn him, after one meeting with someone, that this man or that woman doesn't like you, that he or she boded him no good, and all he would do would be to laugh it off or say I was exaggerating. But invariably I would turn out to be right. Although I tried to keep my gift to myself, I could not — I would eventually show it to the person, either in my attitude or in some sudden, pointed remark or barbed witticism that I really did not intend to make. I was, of course, trying to protect him, but when I saw that he simply did not possess the perspicacity to see what I was doing for him, I gave up.

Furthermore, I gave up for good. Today I never use my gift any more. I have put it away and locked it up in a closet, so to speak, along with many other troubles of the past. But I know just as surely as I am sitting here that right now, if I wanted to, I could take out my gift, dust it off and use it again. . . . It may be a little rusty but it is still loaded.

If the problems involved in getting rid of the Duchess' husband No. 1 were not easy ones, those involved in getting rid of husband No. 2 were no walk in the park either. His name was Ernest Aldridge Simpson, and he would soon be legendary in English song and story — in the latter, for being known as "The Unimportance of Being Ernest," in the former, for being starred in a revised Christmas carol of the day:

> *Hark, the herald angels sing,*
> *Mrs. Simpson pinched our King.*

Actually Ernest was only half English — he was also half American. On his eighteenth birthday, however, when asked by his father, who was English, to declare himself one way or the other, he declared for being English. Once having so declared, in short order Ernest soon went all the way and later when the Duke, first as Prince of Wales and later as King, began coming regularly to the Simpson house in Bryanston Court, he seemed to have thoroughly subscribed to the good old-fashioned English belief that when the King comes to your house, he not only sits in your place at the head of the table, he also owns everything including, if he wants her, your wife. Indeed, in Ernest's case, when the time came for divorce Ernest not only went out of his way to make himself guilty with the necessary adultery evidence but also seemed, as he always did, to go the second mile. Indeed what he did was to perform the adultery with one of the Duchess' closest friends, whom he afterwards married.

In short order we assigned Ernest a long list of standard English faults — most of them, I was pleased to point out to the Duchess, began, like "standard" itself, with "st" — stuffiness, stuck-upness, stubbornness, and stodginess — most of which were not very fair, because while Ernest was hardly a life-of-the-party type neither was he, to use one more "st," a stick-in-the-mud. A relatively successful man in the shipping business in both America and Britain, he was an excellent host and a congenial, if quiet, guest. From the Duchess' point of view we could not, of course, get into the real fault he had — which was being happily married to someone else.

The latter was an American woman, whom I eventually had the opportunity to meet in person. I asked her to tell me what she thought of the Duchess. She replied, with a wry smile, "The Duchess," she said, "was a very helpful woman. First she helped herself to my apartment and then she helped herself to my clothes, and then she helped herself to my husband." I was also privileged to have, some years later, a particularly memorable meeting with the husband in question. It occurred at a cocktail party in New York, when a man came up to me and said, "I thought you might like to talk to me. My name is Ernest Simpson."

I did indeed enjoy our talk. It was not a long one, but it was long enough for me to learn that the Duchess' version of her life with Ernest was by no means the only one. There was also the matter of his version. And this was, in a word, that there was hardly a word of truth in hers. "She had a terrible temper," Mr. Simpson said quietly. "I really think the Duke was mortally afraid of her. I know most of the time I was."

Almost everyone, to this day, has his or her own opinion of the abdication of King Edward VIII. So much so indeed that, looking back on it, I sometimes think that even Polar Bear, had he been alive at that time, would have had his opinion on it, too. He was, for one thing, a terrific little abdicator. He could abdicate from a party at the drop of a hat — sometimes literally, in fact, at the drop of a hat. He could also abdicate from where I wanted him to be if he had the slightest suspicion that there might be, in the offing, either a pill, an examination of an ear, a bath, or even a toenail cut. He would also abdicate in a split second from the position of being the only possible perpetrator of some kind of total spilling or breakage. One second he would be there, the next he was nowhere to be found.

One thing I believed without any doubt at all, and that is that Polar Bear would not have thought the Windsors played it very smart — and Polar Bear was not only one very smart cat himself, he was also an excellent judge of smartness in both other cats and people. Both the Duke and Duchess liked to tell people that they did not like to talk about the abdication, but this could not have been farther from the truth. Almost every conversation I had with the Duke would have at least one time in it the preface, "When I was King," and then a story about that. As for the Duchess, she did not know the first thing about the British government, nor indeed about the British people. All she knew was how to get a man, and how to get ahead. But when she got both, in the person of the Prince of Wales and then King, and literally got to the head of the class in that department, she was as stubborn as he was in believing everything would turn out the way she wanted it to. The whole trouble about the abdication, she often said to me, was that she and the Duke had no time to organize their defenses, because it all happened so fast.

So fast! According to her, they met late in the fall of 1930. According to the Duke's book, they met in the fall of 1931. I have always thought that it would have been nice if they at least could have gotten together on that fact. But no matter. Whether it was 1930 or 1931, they still had either five or six years — give or take your pick — to figure out what was going to happen. One wonders what they talked about on long winter evenings.

Actually from the first time Prime Minister Baldwin faced the Duke, then King, with the facts of wife about being a British monarch, the die was cast. Ironically, the Royal Marriages Act did not mean that the King could not marry someone who had two living ex-husbands. Constitutionally, in fact, the King was free to marry anyone he liked except a Roman Catholic. All the Royal Marriages Act did was give him the power to prohibit the marriage of any member of his family. But, again, nobody could prohibit the marriage of the King himself. Despite this, on Baldwin's side of the affair he had first of all his Cabinet, who could be counted on not to be enamored with the idea of the Duchess as Queen; second, Parliament, which would certainly react the same way; third, the Dominions, who would have to accede to any such marriage; and fourth and finally, the Church. The Church of England regarded marriage as indissoluble except by death. And although most people in England believed that the monarch was the Head of the Church of England, that was not actually the case. What he was, though, and officially was so designated, was Defender of the Faith. As such, conceivably, he could have been, for making such a marriage, excommunicated. Although this was not likely, the fact was, it was possible. Neither the Duke nor the Duchess was religious. They almost never went to church — and the Duke's relations with the powers-that-be in the Church of England were far from good.

From the beginning the Duke seemed to have no conception of what was ranged against him and, even if he did, stubborn as he was, he was certain he could find a loophole. He particularly persisted in this when the Duchess was with him, staying at Fort Belvedere. When, however, a brick was thrown through a window of the Duchess' home, the Duchess — who was far from a courageous woman — immediately wanted to leave England. In short order she set off, in company with the Duke's equerry, to the home of the Herman Rogerses, friends of hers in Cannes. En route, she stopped from time to time to scream at the Duke over the telephone not to abdicate — which was certainly the last thing she could have wished, or indeed had bargained for.

The Duchess always claimed that Esmond Harmsworth, one of the cabal of British publishers who saw to it that the public never learned about the Duke's dilemma until it was a *fait accompli,* was the first to approach her with the idea of a morganatic marriage. She claimed to me that she had never heard of such a thing. This was, of course, not true — all the Duke's circle had been discussing it for weeks. The *Concise Oxford Dictionary* defines a morganatic marriage as "one between man of exalted rank and woman of lower rank, who remains in her former station." Surely, one hardly needs to reread that definition to know exactly what the Duchess thought about it. Several times, indeed, she expressed herself to me succinctly on this point. "I thought," she said, "it was medieval." Knowing her well by this time, I was not in the least surprised. Having set her cap for a King, she hardly relished the idea of losing the prize when it came so close to her grasp. If she settled for being a morganatic wife, not only would she not be a Queen, she would have settled for something which, to her at least, sounded all too much like being a peasant.

If the Windsors had made a comedy of errors of the abdication, their life afterward came very close to being a farce. Since they could not get married until after the Duchess' Simpson divorce became final — which was not to be for several months — and since they could not either live together or even be seen together during this period for fear of a collusion charge being levelled against the divorce — as if it were not close to a worldwide fact of life that there had been collusion — they chose to live during this period in separate countries. The Duchess remained at Cannes while the Duke chose, of the various places offered to him, the Schloss Engesfeld home of Baron de Rothschild in Austria. And here he stayed for many months while he and the Duchess talked on long distance telephone almost every day, with almost every call being concerned with how furious they both were at his brother, George VI. The Duke had, typically, never given a thought about how difficult the assumption of Kingship would be for his brother, who was a shy, reserved person with a pronounced stammer. From the abdication on, however, he gave a good deal of thought to his brother. I have never forgotten one day when I mentioned something about his brother. The Duke interrupted me. "That stuttering idiot," he said.

As for the Duchess, besides calling the Duke on the phone about his brother, she also wrote numerous letters on the subject to him. On one occasion, she even accused him of having an affair with Baroness Rothschild when the Baron had gone away. This was not true, but it is almost a pity it is not. It would at least have proved that the Duke's anti-Semitism, which obviously did not extend to the Rothschilds, also did not extend to matters of the heart.

It did, however, extend to dinner parties after he and the Duchess were back together again and entertaining in

Paris. On one occasion, he amazed an English friend when the subject of Hitler came up. "I have never thought," the Duke said to the man, "Hitler was such a bad chap." As for myself, I have never forgotten one of the very fanciest dinners I ever attended at the Windsors'. From my seat of some distance to the Duke, I heard the Duke, who was at that time drinking rather heavily, talking loudly to the lady on his left. He was talking loudly enough so that not only did I hear, but so did several other people. The talk between him and the lady was clearly about Hitler, and also clearly involved a disagreement.

Suddenly the Duke took both the lady's hands in his and, closing her fingers together, enclosed his hands over them. By now most of us were watching in amazement, but either because of how loudly they were talking or because of what they were doing with their hands, there occurred one of those curious silences which sometimes happen even at a large table. Suddenly the Duke said to the lady — and very clearly — "You just don't understand. The Jews had Germany in their tentacles. All Hitler tried to do was free the tentacles." With that, he released the lady's hands.

For a very long moment there was literally not a sound at the table. Then, very quietly, a man spoke. "Sir," he said, "with all due respect, I never believed I would ever hear, at a civilized dinner table, a defense of Adolf Hitler."

The Duke turned red but said nothing. Neither, for some time, did anybody else. After the dinner I went over to the man who had said that and it turned out he was Milton Biow, an extremely prominent New York advertising man. I told him that in all the time I had worked with the

Windsors, in my opinion what he had said took more courage than I had seen exhibited by anyone I had ever met in their house.

To be around any couple in which one partner, be it the male or the female, is totally dominant, is not a pleasant experience. In the case of the dominance of the Duchess over the Duke, however, the fawners and the hangers-on, the sycophants and the social climbers, did not seem upset by it. To them, the Windsors were, after all — or at least one of them was — royalty, and for them this was enough. But for anyone with even a modicum of taste or objectivity, the repeated evidence of the Duchess' dominance was so infuriating that at times one could not help feeling sorry for the Duke. One soon realized, though, that this was hardly necessary for the simple reason that he did not just put up with it, he actually liked it. Even Polar Bear could not have stood it — he would have known that a cat could look at a king, but in this case he would certainly have wondered why it was worth it.

The very first working day I had with the Duchess was one on which I saw for the first time this dominance, and I never forgot it. We were having tea and talking about the book when the Duke suddenly wandered in, tea cup in hand. Immediately he started talking about how he and his ghostwriter had worked. Equally immediately the Duchess stepped in. "We're not talking about *your* book," she said, "we're talking about my book. Take your tea in the other room." As I watched him go, I thought of two things — how much he had given up, and then to be treated like that, and also if she spoke to him like that with a relative stranger present — one who, after all, would one day be writing about her — then how did she talk to him when they were alone?

To some extent this question was answered by the Duchess' Aunt Bessie, who was with her almost from the beginning of her courtship by the Duke. She was also with her as a guest at Fort Belvedere during the crucial days of the abdication crisis. On one occasion, after a dinner party, when the other guests had gone the Duchess berated the Duke — who was, after all, now King — about something he had done and continued this berating to such an extent that he finally burst into tears. Later, after the Duchess had gone to her room, Aunt Bessie sat with the Duke for some time, not only commiserating with him but definitely taking an anti-Duchess side of their whole relationship. "You can always get another woman to love," she said. "But you can't get another throne." It was good advice but, unfortunately, like most good advice the Duke received, he did not take it.

By the time the summer was up I had had all of the Windsors I could take. And, if I may be pardoned the expression, I abdicated — and I never regretted the decision. After leaving the job, I sailed back to the U.S. on the same *Queen Mary* I had sailed over on. In New York, after we docked, several reporters came on board — some of whom, since the story of my leaving the Duchess' book had preceded me, had various questions for me. One question, however, they all had — why did I leave the job? I told them I could not make the Duchess of Windsor into Rebecca of Sunnybrook Farm.

I think this satisfied them, but it did not satisfy a young lady who had overheard it. "I don't care what you say," she said, "she got a king, didn't she?"

I had an answer for that, too, but unfortunately the young lady did not wait to hear it. I wanted to tell her that yes, she was right, the Duchess had gotten a king. But I felt the young lady should also know that it had not been all that terrific. And, besides that, I wanted to tell her that I now thought England should put up a monument to the Duchess. She was, after all, responsible for the country getting a change of monarchy just when it needed it most — before the Second World War.

If I had had a chance, I would also have liked to tell her that what the country lost was a man without character or courage, let alone sense of duty, who thought nothing of giving up his throne to a shy and gentle man who was ill-fitted for the job, who stammered, and for whom every public appearance was a painful one.

This is what they lost, I would have told the young lady. And what they got in return was a man who overcame all his difficulties to become one of the greatest wartime leaders in British history.

Surely the woman responsible for that deserved at least a small monument. Even Polar Bear would have seen the reason for that.

If my Windsor ghostwriting experience was a major error in my life and, as "September Song" has it, a plentiful waste of time, it was shortly followed by another error which was also major, and was an even more plentiful waste. And again, like the Windsor debacle, I believe that if Polar Bear had been in the picture, it would not have happened.

Actually, my only excuse is that the first error led directly into the second. What happened was, coming back on the *Queen Mary* from the Windsor story, I had some long, long thoughts — not only about the Windsors in particular, but also about Society in general. Having seen, almost nauseatingly firsthand, what passed for Society in the form of the aforementioned fawners and hangers-on around the Windsors, I became more and more convinced that the word "Society" itself was suspect — that whatever it once was, it certainly was not anymore, and that something new might not be any better but it could hardly be, at worst, worse.

I decided, in a word, that what had supplanted the word "Society" in at least the media world of a new day was the word "Celebrity." With that in mind, I decided to do some research on the subject. And, I soon discovered, that once upon a time there was a day when the word "Celebrity" was used only impersonally — that a person might be said to have celebrity, or fame, but it would have been as meaningless to say "A Celebrity" as it would have been to say "A Fame."

I also discovered that the change in the word as it had come to be used was by no means as modern as most people assume. As far back as 1836, for example, the *American Quarterly Review*, speaking of John Jacob Astor I, declared, "From an obscure stranger he had made himself into one of the 'celebrities' of the country." This was still early enough, it is true, for the word to be used with quotation marks, but what was particularly interesting to me was that it was used in connection with a man whose family would soon become pillars, if not particularly stable ones, of New York Society.

All of which led me to two further observations — the first one being that Society clearly started as Celebrity, but then, in at least some cases, continued as Society, and the second one was that, whatever it was, again in a few cases, it continued on to become Aristocracy. In any case, as far back as 1856, I found no less a "celebrity" than Emerson himself using the word, and without quotation marks, in *English Traits*. And, finally, by the turn of the century, as witnessed by a 1908 article in *Harper's Bazaar* entitled "The Dinner Party," the word was in full flower:

> If one wishes to invite the Van Aspics in order to impress another guest, one must first find someone to impress the Van Aspics. One must find, then, a celebrity.

The question then became, of course, which was more important — the world of the Van Aspics or the world of the celebrities? For a while it seemed, in fact for half a century, the Van Aspics and the celebrities would, in a sense, split the pie — they were both deemed important. But, as time went on, however, there was no question but that the celebrities had overwhelmed the Van Aspics.

Not that Society died easily — it did not. For years it had been carefully tended and looked after, and was finally even given the crowning accolade of being numbered. Since this was exactly what I was proposing to do with celebrities, I took some interest in who these numberers were. And, as it turned out, I should have taken a lot more interest because an extremely smarmy lot they were — and hardly a lot one would wish to join.

The first and most famous of these was a curious Southern gentleman named Ward McAllister. Born in Savannah, Georgia, and married to an heiress, he soon came to New York and attached himself to the then-reigning The Mrs. Astor. Since Mrs. Astor's ballroom held just four hundred people, Mr. McAllister took it upon himself to decide, in 1888, that Society should consist of just that number, thereby giving birth to the famous phrase "The Four Hundred." In explaining this, however, Mr. McAllister invariably went back to Mrs. Astor's ballroom. "If you go outside that number," he said, "you strike people who are either not at ease in a ballroom or else make other people not at ease." Sometimes, though, as Mr. McAllister later admitted, for, as he put it, a large ball, it was possible to go outside what he called "the exclusive, fashionable set" and invite "professional men, doctors, lawyers, editors, artists and the like." But, Mr. McAllister stated sternly, he did not advise doing this often, and in fact recommended it "primarily for New Year's Eve."

Hard on the heels of "Mr. Make-A-Lister," as Mr. McAllister, in his last years, was called, came another numberer named Mr. Louis Keller. Whereas Mr. McAllister had been relatively striking looking, with a Van Dyke beard and odd and rather loud clothes, his successor, Mr. Keller, the son of a New Jersey patent lawyer, was in person extremely unprepossessing. Sandy-haired, with a curious-looking, drooping mustache, and a squeaky, affected voice, he was troubled early in life with deafness — an affliction which seemed to ward off, at least from his point of view, some of the criticism he received for the sole distinction of his life — which was to found the *Social Register*. Growing up on the fringe of Society, Mr. Keller was, like so many numberers and arbiters before him and since, fascinated by it. "The mind of Louis Keller," said one biographer, "never went beyond Society."

Mr. Keller actually got his start by publishing the Society gossip sheet called *Town Topics* — one which proved a predecessor to the latter-day gossip columns. Nor was Mr. Keller by any means the first to publish a listing of Society. There had, in fact, been a host of "Blue Books," as they were called, or "Visiting Lists," before his *Register*. Mr. Keller, however, had two important things going for him: One was that he, as the son of a lawyer, even if just a patent one, knew his way around the law, and somehow managed to protect his *Social Register* from being copied. The other was that he somehow managed to protect himself from large suits which declared that he had copied others — which of course he had.

In any case, by the time of Mr. Keller's death in 1922, his *Social Register* was a success, partly because of its distinctive black-and-red design — one which, in turn, I copied for my book, *Who Killed Society?* Indeed, three weeks after Mr. Keller's death, at the time the ownership had passed to Mr. Charles Beekman, Keller's nephew and heir, the *Register* reached its peak, numbering editions in twenty-one cities. From that time on, however, there was trouble — the start of which was the *Register*'s attempt to invade the South. "Down here," one Richmond lady informed Mr. Beekman, "we know who we are without being told."

The *Register* also met with a similar lack of success when it invaded Minneapolis–St. Paul, and followed this by having to abandon cities like Detroit and Providence for "lack of interest." Nor was it helped when the *Register* found it necessary to combine Philadelphia with Wilmington, and Cleveland with Cincinnati and Dayton. Although Cleveland was later freed of this burden, the *Register* itself, by the 1950's, was down to eleven editions. As was its custom in those days, first they selected a correspondent, then with his or her help chose a thousand or more names, then mailed them all *Registers* with a five-dollar-due bill. Here, and in various other places, the *Register* began having difficulty for its policy of throwing people out because of what the *Register* owners regarded as "poor marriages." This included, among other sins, a gentleman marrying an actress, which often provoked the *Register* to high dudgeon. Even the regular letter one received after a marriage from the so-called "Social Register Association" was something of a stopper, too:

> It has been brought to the Association's attention that Mr. ——— has married recently. Will Mr. ——— therefore kindly inform the Association of the date and place of his marriage and give the full Christian and maiden name of the bride and the names of her parents in order that the customary notice may be entered in the Dilatory Domiciles.
>
> If Mrs. ——— was previously married will Mr. ——— kindly give her former married name and state whether she was a divorcée or a widow and if the latter give the Christian name of her late husband.
>
> The Association would also appreciate receiving some information regarding Mrs. ——— as to her Family background and any other particulars which would be of assistance.

The repetition of the word "Christian," as well as the phrase "Family background," not to mention "Dilatory Domiciles," can be extremely irritating to sensitive bridegrooms, or brides for that matter, and at least half of the newspaper stories about so-and-so being "dropped" for marrying so-and-so could be traced to such simple irritations. The bridegroom just did not return the form, and the *Social Register* staff being what it had always been, the couple was, in the next edition, not present.

The basic way the *Social Register* has always been run is to have correspondents in various cities whose idea of helping the editors in New York as to whom to put in and whom to put out was to clip Society columns and mail them to New York. For many years the Boston correspondent of the *Register* was Mrs. John Jay Attridge. Although a Roman Catholic herself, as was her boss, Mr. Keller, she told me she was more associated with what she called Boston's "Irish political element" than with the "Yankee Social," and yet she had seen her *Register* include, as she told me, "very few Catholics," and, as far as she could recall, "no Jews at all." Mrs. Attridge also told me she received $150 for her first year's work for the *Register* in 1907. In 1975, her fiftieth anniversary, she received, again for the full year, $350. She was, however, philosophical about this. "It came to about a dollar a day at the end," she told me, "and after all, I worked only about two minutes a day."

After a long pause, during which Mrs. Attridge looked at me closely, she told me she had nothing to do with my being dropped from the *Social Register*. She said it had been "handled in New York," and that the editors felt very strongly about the *Register* being criticized, and that she had been told I had definitely criticized it on television. I told her not to worry about it — that somehow I had managed to survive despite being dropped. I did, however, tell her exactly what I had said. I told her it had happened on the old Garroway "Today Show," and what had happened was that Garroway had asked me about the *Social Register*. Since his famous chimpanzee, J. Fred Muggs, was with us, I suggested to Garroway that one way we might understand it was for us to endeavor to get Mr. Muggs into the *Register*. I told him it would not be easy, because Mr. Muggs was in show business, but I would have to know whether or not he was married. Mr. Garroway said he did not know whether he was or not. I told him we would have to get a letter of recommendation from somebody already in the *Register*, and then get him at least five seconding letters. I told him it would take time, but not to worry. If his name was Fred J. Muggs, I said, I doubted it would be possible. But since his name had a nice society sound of J. Fred Muggs, I thought at least we had a chance.

Unfortunately, we failed — Mr. Muggs never made the *Register*. But a young lady friend of mine, using the same tactics we had recommended for Mr. Muggs, did, for one edition at least, manage to get her poodle in. "Pedigreed," she assured me, "of course."

Even this, however, was not my favorite story about the *Register*. That came to me from an assistant editor of *Look* magazine who told me she had been interviewed by two members of the *Register's* secret "Advisory Board" who told her they were a search committee for a replacement editor of the *Register*. The young lady never forgot the experience, although she asked me not to use her name — something which was, I thought, a large tribute to the curious power the *Register* had over people, even those whom one would think would be above such matters. In any case, I respected the young lady's wishes for anonymity, and told her story, without her name, as follows:

> At first, she recalled, the men "beat around the bush" and were very "hush-hush." Then they finally admitted they needed a new editor and also that the office needed modernization; they said they had only one "badly battered typewriter" and that most of the addresses were still done by hand. By this time the young editor was beginning to have strong doubts herself about wanting the job, but she recalls that the men were determined to know everything about her; they even wanted to see her paintings and were vastly relieved, she said, when they learned they weren't abstract. Since she also wrote for *Look*, she naturally brought up the question, if she took the job, of her writing on the "outside." This caused some consternation. The men wanted to know exactly what kind of writing she might be doing. Each thing she mentioned caused increased consternation. Finally in desperation she asked them what kind of writing they thought she could do. "The best thing for you to be," one of the men said reflectively, "would be a lyric poet."

Some years ago the *Social Register* was bought by, of all people, the late Malcolm Forbes, of *Forbes* magazine. To understand just why Mr. Forbes wanted such a controversial investment is hard to understand, unless one knew Mr. Forbes well enough to know how intrigued he was with matters of the social world, and also how limited he was in certain ramifications of such matters. I recall, for example, crossing on the *Queen Elizabeth II* with him, and asking one evening why he bought the *Register*. "Cleveland," he said to me, very earnestly, "I will tell you anything you want to know about any of my business interests, but I will not tell you about that." Obviously, someone had apprised him that the ownership of such a book could hardly be a plus for his other businesses, let alone for his personal relations. In any case, the *Social Register* was eventually sold again. And today, not only is its advisory board still a secret, so is its ownership.

The *Celebrity Register* was, of course, to be a very different book from the *Social Register*. In the first place, it was not to be a "Blue Book," but a "do" book. Actually, we ended up with half a hundred well-known Society names in it, but just as Society had, at least in my opinion, changed from a how-do-you-do Society to a what-do-you-do, so the whole basis of Celebrity Society was not who somebody was, but who somebody is.

I first took the idea to Earl Blackwell, of Celebrity Service fame, under the impression that he was a book publisher. He was not, but it really did not matter because in the end we published the book ourselves. Later, this was done through different publishers — Harper's, and Simon and Schuster also published it — but they did very little better than we did in publishing it ourselves. And this despite the fact that we had an extraordinarily able group writing the thousands of biographies. There was, for example, R. W. Apple, Jr., formerly of the "Huntley-Brinkley Report," and later a distinguished writer for the *New York Times*. There was also the late Hallowell Bowser, general editor of the *Saturday Review*, and also the late James Fixx, also a *Saturday Review* editor and author of many books on running. Then, too, there was Marian Magid, of *Commentary* magazine, and Andrew Sarris, who became a distinguished critic.

To the best of all our abilities, however, we never had anything but trouble about who should have been in the books and who should not. We learned the hard way that one man's celebrity is another man's nobody. Yet the latter man or woman did have his or her celebrities whom the first man would not know if he fell over them. To the football fan, for one example, half a hundred players are celebrities. To the non-fan, there is Joe Namath, Joe Montana, O. J. Simpson, and possibly Lawrence Taylor. To the rock music fan, there are many more than a hundred world-class celebrities. The non-rock fan would be hard put to name a dozen.

In general, we operated on the theory that to be a celebrity a man or a woman must be known outside his or her field. This failed, however, when we realized that there are whole fields of celebrities which, by their very nature, are known all over — television, for example — and at the same time a great many fields which are also, by their very nature, basically local. We were, however, considerably cheered up by our New Orleans correspondent, Tess Craiger, who gave up the job of deciding who should be in the book from New Orleans. "We are all," she wrote us, "internationally famous locally."

Besides speaking of being known outside one's field, we also had to consider if a celebrity had to be known by his or her face. That sounded like an easy solution, until one begins to realize that there are hundreds of people whose names are household words — writers, for example, or artists, or business executives, or even radio personalities — whose faces would not be known off their own front porches.

Finally, we learned the hard way that we had to distinguish between celebrities and what were then called — an expression which has faded somewhat — VIP's. In those days, however, there was a distinct difference. Both have or had the fame which, to begin with, made his or her name. But the celebrity's fame is his or hers alone — an individual thing — while a VIP's is basically positional. The celebrity's name, in fact, should need no qualifying identification — indeed, that is probably the best definition of a celebrity — but the VIP is likely to need the additional clout of being identified with his or her organization. When Polar Bear came along, I would learn that it was possible to be both a celebrity and a VIP — but to do so, it would help to be a VIC, or Very Important Cat.

Generally speaking, however, the world of the celebrity and the world of the VIP are, well, worlds apart. From the moment they get up in the morning — for the VIP, early, for the celebrity, late — to the time when they go to bed at night — the VIP, early, the celebrity, late — their ways of life are so completely different that if they ever meet — which, except for very large and usually charitable events, they rarely do — they would hardly know what to say to each other. And, if they do, they would undoubtedly slip up right in the introductions, because a celebrity is generally a first-name man or woman, the VIP a Mr., Mrs. or Miss — rarely a Ms.

If not for the celebrity is the world of clubs, boardrooms, and directorships, not for the VIP is the world of television, columns, fan mail, and autographs. If not for the celebrity is the Establishment, not for the VIP is the talk show. If not for the VIP is the street recognition, not for the celebrity is an honorary degree. Indeed, if the celebrity gets an honorary degree, it is likely to be from a college whose chief claim to fame is that it gave him or her one.

The world of the celebrity is the world of ups and downs, of big money periods and almost totally broke periods. The world of the VIP is generally smooth, and generally an upward course. Constantly at the mercy of the press, without a screening shield, the celebrity almost literally lives off his mention in the column, his picture in the paper, and his appearance on TV. If the VIP meets the press at all, it will probably be through a press release. The celebrity has his entourage and his hangers-on, but his life is basically disorganized and is basically a last minute one. He or she is rarely alone, and does not like to be. On the other hand, the VIP has a social life which is so well integrated with his business life that it is hard to tell where one leaves off and the other begins.

The celebrity is probably a Democrat, the VIP is probably a Republican. The VIP will read *The Wall Street Journal, Business Week,* and *Forbes,* while the celebrity will read *Variety, People,* and *Hollywood Reporter.*

The VIP is listed in the telephone book — by his office, and even his home number. The celebrity has a constantly changing and unlisted number. And, if to reach the VIP you have to play "Just a moment, put Mr. so-and-so on the line, please," to reach the celebrity you have to go through his agent, and that is worse. And the irony here is that while the VIP's world is the well-ordered one of the formal letter and the thank-you note, the celebrity does nine-tenths of his business and arranges most of his social engagements by phone.

The personal worlds of the VIP and the celebrity are perhaps the farthest apart of all. The former is generally well ordered and organized; the latter, usually messy. The VIP marries once or, at the most, twice; his children go to private schools and enter the same circumscribed world as their parents'. And when, in the end, the VIP goes to his final reward, he does so via a well-planned service at his church or synagogue. The celebrity, on the other hand, is much married, has different children by different wives and, though not at all averse to pushing them, sometimes unwarrantedly, toward show business, usually finds them difficult to handle, and vice versa. And he goes to his final resting place not via church or synagogue but via extravagant eulogies in a funeral home.

Finally, if you can tell a celebrity from a VIP by the length of his hair (longer), by the width of his tie (wider), by the amount of jewelry (more) and by the cash he carries (much more), you can also tell a VIP from a celebrity by the fact that he drinks more and tips less, plays sports better and tells stories worse.

Some years ago, dining on his fabulous yacht *Christina*, I put to Aristotle Onassis the difference between celebrities and VIP's. "I have done some thinking on the subject," Mr. Onassis said, "and I have come to the conclusion that the way a VIP gets to be a celebrity is to get control of the people's playthings. It's a little like children and their toys. You do not become a celebrity by controlling the people's money, their banks, their natural resources, their raw materials — or even, as in my case, by moving their materials, by shipping. If I had remained just a shipping man, I would have remained comparatively obscure. But the moment I bought Monte Carlo, that was something else again. I then controlled one of the people's playthings. I was like a man who owned motion-picture companies, or a television network, or a racetrack, or horses, or a ball team — they are all celebrities. And since I controlled the most famous casino in the world, I became one of the most famous men in the world."

Certainly, Mr. Onassis' theory would be accurate for many celebrities since his time. A Donald Trump, for example, would hardly be a celebrity as a moderately successful second-generation real estate man, but as the builder of Atlantic City casinos, he was a shoo-in. In the same way, George Steinbrenner, as a second-generation and none too successful shipbuilder, was far from celebritydom. As principal owner of the New York Yankees, albeit the least principled in that club's history, he is, like it or not, a celebrity. Indeed, taking Mr. Onassis' theory a step further, and taking a large list of "the people's playthings" to newspapers and television networks, you have a large list of celebrities, all of whom are VIP's also — from the Hearsts and the Howards and the Sulzbergers to the Paleys and the Sarnoffs and the Tisches.

Curiously, the late Mr. Onassis gave us as much trouble as any celebrity in the book because of his demand to see his finished biography. From the beginning, we had decided the biographee would have nothing to do with his or her biography, and the biographers would try to be fair, if not necessarily reverential. However, Mr. Onassis was not content with this policy, and sent four large men to our modest-sized office to demand the copy. I was doing my best to explain our policy when, seeing that I was getting nowhere, I told the men I would be happy to read them the biography of another Greek, if they would like to hear it. It happened that my assistant, Marian, had just completed the biography of Mr. Spyros Skouras, and dutifully, while the men stood glowering, I read the following:

"In bed that night I don' sleep," he recalls, of the day he first heard of CinemaScope. "Then I finally sleep and I dream. I am dreamin' of Egypt, of lions outside the streets, of Bens Hur and the Quin of Seba, of Betsy Grabble in colors. Oh, I had sooch wonderful dream." And, later arising, he welcomed the Chairman of Soviet Russia to his studio's dining room. "I yam a pure boy from Gris," he announced. "Where else but in America would I be standing here?" "I am a poor boy from the Ukraine," Khrushchev, understandably heatedly, replied. "In Russia, I run the whole she-bang."

Born 28 March 1893, in Skourohorian, Greece, Spyros (pronounced "Spear-os") Panagiotis Skouras came to America in 1908, and went to work for a St. Louis hotelman who every dawn played the National Anthem to improve the boy's patriotism. And, married to Saroula Bruiglia (five children), with his two astute brothers, Charlie and George, he prospered. ("My only hobby," he says, "is gins rummy.") When TV came, it was he who organized the campaign "MOVIES ARE BETTER THAN EVER," and it was he who declared, "The critics should not be putting the nails in our coffins." The 1953 premiere of *The Robe* opened a new error in Hollywood, when Skouras backed the first CinemaScope picture with $30 million. ("The dice is cast," he declared. "We have landed in Normandy.") Then, as Cleopater familias, Skouras stood, presumably, at Dunkirk. In the middle of the worst of it he received a call that Indianapolis was on the phone. "Listen," he shrieked, "I got no damn time to talk to no damn Greek."

I never did find out what the men told Mr. Onassis, but I had the feeling when they left they had at least learned from that biography we were not people to irritate unnecessarily. In any case, the only other sinister demand for advance reading of a biography came from no less a personage than the late J. Edgar Hoover. Once again, our office was penetrated — this time by two of Mr. Hoover's assistants, whom I took to be G-men. Just two of them, however, were somehow even more menacing than Mr. Onassis' four. It is hard to realize today — especially in view of the current anti-Hoover writing — just how much nervousness, if not fear, a visit from Mr. Hoover's men inspired in those days. He was, after all, a man whom nine Presidents had not dared to remove.

One thing was certain. The more the men said "The Director says," and "The Director insists," etc., the crosser I got. It was less bravery than bravado, and in the end, when they stormed out of the office — and storm they did — I still was virtually as nervous as I was when they arrived, and felt sure they would come back. But, fortunately for me, they never did.

One other incident — equally, if not even more menacing — remained. This was a telephone call I received at three in the morning the day before the publication of

Celebrity Register from none other than Walter Winchell. Like Mr. Hoover's power, Mr. Winchell's seems, in retrospect, exaggerated. Let me assure you, at that time it could hardly have been exaggerated. No one before him or since ever had the power and influence he had, not only in his daily newspaper column in the *Mirror* but also on his weekly television and radio shows. Like many others in Winchell's heyday, I seemed to know dozens of people who worked for the man — some worked as press agents who, in return for giving him three interesting or amusing items would get one mention of their client in his column. Others worked not as press agents but just as people who gave him anti-items against somebody they disliked. Unlike Mr. Hoover, Mr. Winchell was not totally anti-Liberal, but he was totally anti-Communist and also against anybody he thought was so inclined. Some people he just disliked for no reason at all.

In any case he made very clear, very quickly, his quarrel with me. The *Celebrity Register* included a biography of one of Mr. Winchell's pet hates — the late Ms. Josephine Baker. With biting sarcasm, and in the familiar, nasal rasping voice that staccattoed out each Sunday night "Good evening, Mr. and Mrs. America and all the ships at sea," he told me, with incredibly increasing rage, just what would happen if the *Register* appeared without that biography of Ms. Baker out — that it would not only be the end of the *Register*, it would also be the end of me.

Once more I could take no credit for being, as I look back on it, remarkably calm. It was really because it was so late at night, and I was so tired and sleepy, that I never really got around to realize what I was risking. Indeed, at one point, when he raged, "Have you any idea to whom you are talking?" I told him I did indeed, but I wanted to ask him his reasons for not wanting Ms. Baker in the book. Actually, I knew the reason all too well. Mr. Winchell was a great friend of Sherman Billingsly, owner of the famed Stork Club, and Ms. Baker had come into the Stork Club one night and, according to her, was not served — which, judging from the attitude of Mr. Billingsly, an ex-gangster from Oklahoma, was undoubtedly true.

Indeed, as I began to wake up more, I asked Mr. Winchell if the fact that Ms. Baker was black had anything to do with his opinion. At this he still raged, but I noticed with extreme pleasure that he stuttered somewhat in his reply. I also managed to get in that if we measured every celebrity by who liked them or disliked them as a criterion for our book, we would have no book at all. Finally, I somehow managed not to resist telling Mr. Winchell that the opening night book party for the *Celebrity Register* would be held at the Stork Club, and I looked forward to seeing him there. I like to think that, in the end I, not he, slammed down the phone. But in all fair retrospect, I now think it was he.

Winchell or no Winchell, the first edition of the *Celebrity Register,* including a biography of Josephine Baker, had its debut at the Stork Club. And the book was, in the beginning, an extraordinary success. It was, however, basically a Tiffany item — in fact, Tiffany's was one of the first stores to ask for it, and sold hundreds of copies. But it was not similarly successful elsewhere, even though we did our best to get it to the bookstores which asked for it, and even though it went through several editions.

To find the reason for this overall lack of success, I can

only recall the story of Joseph Choate, certainly one of New York's most famous legal celebrities, who was once asked to contribute to a fence for a very social cemetery. Mr. Choate refused on the firm grounds that no fence was needed. "No one who is out," his argument claimed, "wants to get in, and no one who is in wants to get out." The *Celebrity Register*, it turned out, was to be just the opposite of that cemetery. People who were out, and thought they should be in — of whom there were thousands — were utterly furious with the book. And the people who were in were almost equally furious, because the biographies were so less glowing than the stuff to which their publicity people had accustomed them.

As if this were not enough, all of us who had anything to do with the book soon learned a basic truth about human nature, which was perhaps best stated by two extremely celebrated authors, Mark Twain and Somerset Maugham. "There's always something about your success," Twain once said, "that displeases even your best friends." And Mr. Maugham put it just as strongly: "All of us like to see our friends get ahead," he said, "but not too far." I could see Polar Bear agreeing with both those statements, even though you could count the number of cat friends he had on the toes of one of his paws.

We could, of course, find solace in just how ridiculous the whole question of fame could be. This was, perhaps, best illustrated when a columnist during World War II, albeit not Mr. Winchell, took a poll to find the "world's favorite personality." The Pope (Pius XII) finished behind Bing Crosby and Frank Sinatra. Others, in order, were Eisenhower, Father Flanagan, MacArthur, Winchell, Sister Kenny, and Bob Hope. Joseph Stalin finished fifteenth.

We could find solace too when, translated to show-business terms, the story becomes that of Kim Novak, who had just made a film for Columbia Pictures. Arriving in Paris she was driven by a chauffeur who told her he had had many other celebrities in his cab. "I have driven Gloria Swanson," he said, "and Cary Grant, and President Coty. I have even driven your President."

"What!" exclaimed Ms. Novak, delightedly. "Harry Cohn!"

CHAPTER FIVE

Polar Bear and Me and Your TV — Your Guide to the Medium Medium

The Windsors and the celebrities were not the only occupants of my attention in the days before Polar Bear. There was also, and almost right up to the time he came to me, the matter of a whole new job — one being something which I had never really wanted to be — a critic.

It is not that I do not like critics — indeed, when they like something I have written I am inordinately fond of them. It is, rather, that I just never wanted to be one myself.

When I was a columnist for the *Saturday Review*, I remember a sign the editor of that magazine, the late Norman Cousins, kept on his desk. "The Critic," the sign said, "Judges Himself in His Criticism."

I admit that sign made me somewhat nervous, but it did not actually stop me from writing any criticism. Like most authors of books, I was occasionally given a book to review for a newspaper's book review section, and when I wrote one of these I certainly did not let that sign make me think that all the time I was writing that criticism what I was really doing was judging myself. Rather, I always thought of that sign as being more like what I have always thought of the New England conscience — that it did not stop you from doing what you shouldn't, it just stopped you from enjoying it.

As I said, I did not know Polar Bear at that time. But as soon as I did know him, I decided that he would have been a terrific critic, if for no other reason than because it never would have crossed his set little mind that all the time he was criticizing something — which, frankly, was most of the time — that what he was really doing was judging himself.

Come to think of it, I have never known a cat who was not at least part critic, and in Polar Bear's case he was so far from being a part critic that even saying such a thing does him a complete injustice — he was a total critic. Frankly, I believe he was born that way, and although I did not know him when he was a kitten, because he was a stray and was at least one year old when I rescued him, I venture to say, without fear of contradiction even from him, that he was a critic even then. Indeed, although some kittens do not open their eyes until they have reached the incredible age of ten days old, I frankly can, even now in my mind's eye, see Polar Bear during that ten-day period raising an eyebrow, even if he could not raise an eye, at the actions of one of his brothers or sisters. And by the time those ten days were up, and he could actually open his eyes, I would not, from this criticism, exempt even his mother.

Of course, when it came to yours truly, the record will show that Polar Bear was critical of me from the moment he first laid eyes on me or rather, specifically, the moment I grabbed him through the fence on that snowy Christmas Eve a score of years ago. This time there was no raised eyebrow, either. What he did was deal me a straight left cross — he always had a better left cross than a right cross — to my jaw.

From that very moment I knew he was not just a future critic but one to be reckoned with, and I assure you he did not, ever since that time, fail my assessment. Take, for example, that first night when I had taken him back to my apartment and he had disappeared, and neither Marian nor I could find him. In fact nobody could find him, although it was not a very large apartment, until my brother, who had just joined the search and was a very thorough person, dismantled the dishwasher. And there, sure enough, hiding at the bottom, was Polar Bear. Although my brother was one of the three men in the Army in World War II who had ever gone all the way from being a private to being general, and although I assure you he could give and take criticism with the best of them, I very much doubt if he ever received in either his military or his civilian life any more telling criticism than that wary, one-eyed, fishy look he received that night from Polar

Bear. Indeed, I can still remember my brother looking first at that look of Polar Bear's and then at me. "What you have here," he said sternly, "is one very critical cat."

Actually, Polar Bear's criticism of me that I remember best happened the very next day when I went to give him a bath. In Polar Bear's firm opinion no one gave cats baths, cats gave themselves baths, and the look he gave me was so critically expressive that it all but spelled out words. "Wash a cat!" I was sure he was saying. "Boy, have I got my work cut out for me with this one!" If the look was not enough, I also remember that along with it, and still some time before the bath, we went eyeball-to-eyeball — he at six inches and me at six-foot-three. I knew immediately, with the kind of criticism he was giving me, it was going to be a question of who blinked first.

Of course you remember what happened. Although the purist might say that he won the first round, and that I blinked first, the fact is that criticism or no criticism, that blink of mine was really a way of avoiding another left cross. And, after all, and again criticism or no criticism, I did give him a bath.

I did not, however, I admit, fare so well the next time I went *mano a mano* with him. This occurred when I began the process of — well, how do I say it — training him. The problem was that, being a newcomer to cat ownership, I must have given him the distinct impression that I thought he was a dog. In any case, I soon learned that there was one thing Polar Bear surely was not, and that was a dog. Actually, I had never really thought of such a thing, but when he was in a critical frame of mind he did not give me the benefit of the doubt for the simple reason that when he had that critical mind of his made up there was no doubt anywhere in it. All I had wanted, after all, was for him to learn the meaning of the word "come." I knew he would not do it, of course — I had already had him long enough for that — but I did hope, however, that at our very first training lesson he might somehow begin to grasp the basic meaning of the word.

I really never did know whether he had ever learned the meaning of the word or not. All I know is that once I said it, the jig was up. He never wanted to hear it again. Eventually we came to a compromise. I was allowed to ask where he was — "Where is Polar Bear?" — after which there would be a suitable interval — a very suitable interval, I would say. In this he would first sit up, and then start to walk and look around and do whatever else crossed his mind, and then finally continue the journey to me. All of this, mind you, only after it had been made totally clear to me that he was coming only entirely by his own volition. Otherwise, of course, he would have to turn in his union card as a cat.

There were so many other times when he was the consummate critic. There was, for one example, my naming him. I never in his entire life knew whether or not he knew his name, let alone whether he liked it. All I ever knew was he liked even less all the other names I had tried and looking back at some of them — like Whitey and Snowball and Snowflake — I hardly blamed him. Another example of his consummate artistry at the craft of being a critic was the whole episode of my giving him a pill — particularly what I thought was my final victory, when I had grabbed him, shoved open his mouth, popped in the pill, shut his mouth, and then stroked his throat over and over, until I was certain there was not the slightest possibility that he had not swallowed the pill. Only then to see, of course, a bare few moments later, when I was savoring my victory and reminding him what had been won in a fair and open fight, out of the corner of my eye, a tell-tale little white object in the rug behind me. Which was, of course, what you had guessed it was.

Most critics are not known for their smiles, but one I will never forget was the smile Polar Bear gave me after that pill episode. It came after I looked first at the pill and then, slowly, back at him while all the time he was doing exactly what I was doing — first looking at the pill and then, just the way I had done looking back at him, only this time he looked back at me. And if it is possible that a cat's smile could reach from ear to ear — well, that is exactly what his smile, slowly but steadily, did.

One thing I did not make clear, and that was the nature of the job I had undertaken before I had Polar Bear. It was, not to beat around the bush, the job of being a critic of television for, of all magazines, *TV Guide*. But after the job was mercifully over, and Polar Bear had come to me, I often wondered what kind of critic of television he would have been. He would not, of course, have been one as thorough as I was. After all, I had to see each show three times before writing about it, and I do not believe his attention span would have been up to that. Indeed, Polar Bear's attention span at watching television is the shortest I have ever seen for anything except when I was talking to him about something which was very important, for his own good, for him to hear.

It is true there were very few things on television of which he was very fond. One of these was Ping-Pong.

Since Ping-Pong, however, comes on in full force on your TV only once every four years, during the Olympics, it really was not the answer to seeing whether or not he would be a better critic than I was.

Readers with long memories will recall that at one time I even went so far as to try to train Polar Bear for watching television. Training Polar Bear for anything, as I have already pointed out, was not easy, but to train him for watching television was something else again. For one thing, you had to train him to watch it, and before he would do that you had to train him to like it, for the simple reason that he would not do anything he did not like to do unless you were right there to hold him, preferably with both hands around his neck. With that in mind I bought some television videos which were specially produced for training cats to watch television — which certainly seemed a pretty limited field, but everyone to his or her own business, I always say. Anyway, as I have previously written somewhere — I cannot remember where — the most curious of these, put out by PetAvision, came in three sections entitled, in order, "Cheep Thrills," "Mews and Feather Report," and "A Stalk in the Park."

I really could not believe those titles. Sex and violence — there they were, out in the open, and even on cat video where any kitten could see them, and probably right on the mews — or rather, news — and even in any kind of feather, or weather, or whatever.

In any case, even if for the purpose of making Polar Bear a television critic, I certainly did not want to corrupt him. There was, after all, enough sex and violence in everyday life in New York City without subjecting him to any more of it — and particularly on his own Cat TV, which I had to pay for. I did find, however, as I have also mentioned previously, another offering called "Kitty Video" which was put out by Lazy Cat Productions. In this was a pamphlet entitled. "How to Teach Your Cat to Watch TV." "Most cats," this began, "are not accustomed to watching television, and will need some assistance to learn this human skill."

Human *skill* — they had to be kidding, but they were not. Indeed, the pamphlet went on to warn about distractions — loud music, too many people in the room, and other animals — all of which, they said, could "cause a lack of concentration on the cat's part."

With that I surely agreed — it could be a problem. Polar Bear's concentration span, with the exception of when it was addressed to the pigeons on my balcony or something like that, was, if anything, even shorter than his attention span. And, when instruction was involved, particularly with me doing the instruction, it was close to zero. In any case, to get around distractions, the pamphlet advised never forcing a cat to watch TV but rather, and apparently casually, placing him in your lap and then positioning his head toward the television screen. "Strategically," the pamphlet suggested, "scratch under the right cheek to aim head left."

That, frankly, I was never able to accomplish. Nor did I have any better luck with another suggestion the pamphlet had which it said was highly recommended. "Tapping gently on the TV screen, " it stated, "can help bring a cat's attention to the video." I tried this with Polar Bear, but it was no easier this time when I tried to teach him to be a TV critic than it was when I tried to do it just to teach him to watch for the fun of it. I learned that Polar

Bear was already a critic of TV, and already such a stern critic that he wanted no more of it — or else he felt put down by having to watch special cat TV. I always felt Polar Bear infinitely preferred doing something that was not meant for him to do rather than doing something that was.

One thing the pamphlet insisted on was that I should keep close watch on him while all this was going on. In fact, the "Kitty Video" pamphlet had a stern injunction about this, which went as follows:

> Do not leave your cat alone while the video is playing. If the cat should leap at the screen, it could cause damage both to furnishings and to the cat. Your cat must learn to watch TV passively. With practice, your cat can become a harmless couch potato.

Again, I remind you I had been through all this before. And if the first time I had been through it I had said I was not at all sure I had wanted him to be a couch potato, let alone a harmless one that time, the second time, when the job was, after all, to make him a critic of TV, I felt that even if he was going to be a couch potato I would have preferred a little toughness about it.

Curiously, I found that getting Polar Bear to watch what I wanted him to watch on TV was very much like the difficulty I had always had in this regard with Marian. Time after time, when I wanted Marian to watch something I was watching, or watch something I was supposed to be watching but could not because there was a ball game on at the same time or something else I wanted to watch, I found that she just would not do it. She would say that she wanted to watch what she wanted to watch —

which was so thoughtless and selfish of her that though I am a very long-suffering person I have felt it very difficult to deal with.

One day, however, I had a chance to redress those wrongs I had so patiently undergone. I happened to be at Marian's apartment that day when the TV repairman came to repair the remote control. While he was busy either trying to fix it or preparing to sell her another, it suddenly occurred to me to ask him if it would be possible for me to get a remote control for her set which would work from my apartment. It was, after all, a perfectly reasonable request. There were many times when I would see something on TV that I wanted her to see — and right away too — and sometimes there was not even time to call. What I wanted her to look at would be all over by the time I called. Instead, what I wanted was the kind of remote control by which, if she was watching something else on another channel, I could immediately change her set to the channel I wanted her to see. And, if she wasn't watching anything, I could immediately turn her set on to what I wanted her to watch.

I repeat, it was a perfectly reasonable request, and I even pointed out to the man that there were probably thousands if not hundreds of thousands of men who would want the same thing — to have their women friends watch something they were watching. It could, I told him, be a terrific business for the TV people, but the man was not smart enough to see the possibilities. All he did was look first at Marian and then at me as if to say he simply did not believe what he had just heard. Honestly, he never even did me the courtesy of giving me an answer to my request. Some people, it seems, just do not realize when they have been given a great idea on a silver platter.

Even Marian did not seem to understand what a great idea it was. She seemed to take the repairman's side. And, if all this was not hard enough for me to take, there was a postscript to it. A couple of weeks later when I was at my apartment watching a cable channel, all of a sudden a movie came on. It was a new movie, too, a Pay-Per-View one. Very excitedly, I called Marian and told her what had happened — that I was apparently going to get to see a new Pay-Per-View TV movie for nothing.

Then, if you please, Marian explained that it was not quite like that. "You are not going to see it for nothing," she said. "You *are* paying for it. I found out I could order it just by giving them your phone number." At this Marian paused, the way she always does. "It's just like that re-mote-control thing you wanted," she said, "only they already have this one."

Not content with simply doing something awful like that, Marian also has to have the last word, too. Fortu-nately, as I have said before, and undoubtedly will have to say again, I have the patience of Job.

All in all, what Polar Bear and I were most of the time reduced to watching were shows which television never had anything to do with — except years later to put them on — old movies. Night after night we would see an old movie, sometimes for the umpteenth time, and never once think of turning it off just because we had seen it so many times before. After all, we had to make sure it came out the same way it always did. Curiously, Polar Bear's and my preoccupation with old movies reminded me of something which had happened long before Polar Bear came to me, at about the time I took on the job of television criticism. It was a statement made by Mr. Mike Dann, at that time vice-president in charge of programming for CBS. "The biggest trouble facing television today," Mr. Dann opined, "is that we are running out of old movies."

Needless to say, this was grist for my mill. Feeling that Mr. Dann had no right to say something like that and then leave us, in the face of that terrible news, with no actual facts, I resolved to take issue with him. Tell us, Mr. Dann, I pleaded both in print and even on the air, just how many old movies we have left. Tell us exactly the number. The American public, I reminded him, had always been able to bear up under terrible news. It had never been found wanting. But, I stated firmly, it had only been able to bear up and not be found wanting when it had been given the facts. And not just some of the facts, but all of the facts. Then and only then, I pointed out, did the American public measure up. They had measured up at Valley Forge, they had measured up in the War of 1812 when the British burned Washington — the city, not George — they had measured up in the Civil War, on both sides, and they had even measured up in the Blizzard of '88 — not 1988, I pointed out, but 1888.

But, I also wanted to make clear to Mr. Dann, the American public had measured up only when it had been given all the facts, and in this new trial this was the least Mr. Dann owed us. Without another day's delay he should tell us just exactly how many old movies we had left. No matter how bad the news, he must give it to us. The truth, the whole truth, and nothing but the truth. And then, once we had that truth, we could start to cut down. We would not, of course, overdo and cut out watching old movies altogether — that would just make us sick. We would cut down slowly. First, we should figure out just how many old movies we watched each week and, whatever that number was, the next week we would watch one old movie less. We would, say, just watch one old movie less in the late afternoon or in the late evening and finally, after nine or ten weeks of cutting down one at a time, we would not watch any old movie at all. We would not even watch Jimmy Stewart in *It's a Wonderful Life*, or John Wayne in *The Quiet Man*. Of course we could, in those cases, if it made us feel better, just turn them on and then turn the sound off and say them to ourselves. It would not be hard. After all, we knew them by heart.

Interestingly, I found, watching with Polar Bear, that just about the only TV which received his full attention was the cat commercials. Short as these were, he watched them and listened to them intently — and even became, in his way, a full-fledged critic of them. How could I tell? It was easy. He either sniffed at them or shook his head. I soon realized what it was, and I had been right about him being, in his way, a critic of them. What he was, was jealous of them — and right to the very depths of his green eyes.

Immediately, I tried to get him to understand that jealousy was a very bad trait in a critic. A critic, I tried to point out to him, had to rise above wondering how he or she would be in an acting part or a commercial or anything else, and must instead compare the performance seen only to the ideal, and certainly not the personal. I did not think Polar Bear grasped this very well. He was just not any good at grasping what he didn't want to grasp — in fact he was awful at it.

Of course, to be fair there were certain animal shows which, if they did not go overboard on dogs, would keep his attention for a while, if not his concentration. But the average, run-of-the-mill television show, I noticed, held very little appeal for him. And, curiously, at the same time I noticed this, I also noticed they held very little appeal for me. Furthermore, all the time I was watching television with Polar Bear to see how he would be as a critic, I was at the same time making a comparison, not only of me as a critic compared to him, but also how the average shows were compared to the average show I had, for some fourteen years, from 1963 through 1976, been reviewing in *TV Guide*. And, frankly, this comparison was easy — generally speaking, those new shows I was watching with Polar Bear were not only not better than the ones I had been reviewing, they were actually worse. And the very worst thing about the comparison was that it held true even when the recent shows were practically carbon copies of the ones I had reviewed.

This comparison could even be carried right to today, as I write this. Take, for example, one of the most popular of today's comedies, "Murphy Brown." This show, obviously deeply indebted to the old "Mary Tyler Moore Show," is nowhere near as well-written, as believable, or as funny as that one was. Even leaving out any comparison between the two stars, compare for a moment the over acting and over active supporting actors from "Murphy Brown" with those, say, of the peerless Ted Baxter of the "Mary Tyler Moore Show" of yesterday.

Today's endless talk and crime shows — sometimes it is hard to tell which is which — are probably the best examples of television not improving. Take, for example, the best crime shows of yesterday. It would seem easy to carbon copy "Columbo," "Kojak," "Ironsides," etc. But obviously it has not been easy for the networks to do so. They cannot seem to do it even when they actually copy the shows with the same characters. Indeed, with exactly the same Peter Falk, today's "Columbo" scripts are a far cry from what they were in the old days, as is the case with Telly Savalas' scripts with "Kojak," or "Perry Mason," or "Ironsides" with the same Raymond Burr. Indeed, about the only shows you can count on to keep the same quality they were when I was reviewing them are actual repeats — say, of shows all the way from "The Honeymooners" to "All in the Family."

This is not to say there have not been efforts made in the quality direction. Notably, the "Civil War" series, not to be confused with "Civil Wars," the network situation comedy. But unfortunately, these are few and far between, and perhaps even more unfortunately, most of them, like the great shows in the days when I was reviewing — like "The Forsythe Saga" or "Upstairs, Downstairs" — were British imports. As for what has happened to TV news, with the exception of PBS's "MacNeil-Lehrer News Hour," it has gone almost steadily downhill. Not so much the three evening network newscasts themselves as what has happened to the total corruption around them, with its barrage of curious efforts like "Real Story," "A Current Affair," "Hard Copy," and "Unsolved Mysteries," all of which seem to have had only one recommendation and that is that they were, next to talk shows, the obviously cheapest thing to produce — something which, watching them, is only too amply demonstrated.

And yet even these are not the worst of all the modern shows. That dubious honor I would reserve for the mini-series and the so-called "movies made for television." Actually, all anyone who thought that television in general had improved had to do was to be around at the end of 1992 and the beginning of 1993 when not one or two but all three major networks outdid themselves in trying to put on a movie about a seventeen-year-old prostitute who shot in the face the wife of a man she said was her lover. Afterwards, when their ratings were found to have gone through the roof, virtually all network executives, who had climbed all over each other to put that trash on the air expressed, of all emotions, shock. "I don't know anyone in the business," said the vice-president of movies for NBC, "who wasn't stunned."

But not so stunned, of course, as not to do it again. Indeed, not long before television had reached that nadir of taste, an equally extraordinary event happened in the industry — which occurred when one of the largest cable television companies announced that they would soon be able to supply, on one person's set, five hundred channels. Considering the fact that at the time they said this an entire network could not adequately supply just one channel with twenty-four hours of reasonably watchable fare, the idea of saying they were about to supply five hundred channels was not even mind-boggling, it was just plain boggling, with no mind involved.

*   *   *

Looking back to my *TV Guide* days, when I first met with Mr. Merrill Panitt, the then editor of the magazine, I learned that he had chosen me to be his critic because he liked several book reviews I had done for the *New York Times*. I told him firmly that I felt there was a large difference between a book review for the *New York Times* and a TV review for *TV Guide*, but he would not hear of it. Instead, he preferred to tell me how huge my audience would be — in fact, the more he talked about the circulation of the magazine, the more it sounded as if there were more people who read *TV Guide* every week than there were people. Maybe some of them, I suggested, forgot they already had it and go out and buy it again. He ignored this. Instead, he promised me that after I had worked for *TV Guide* only a short time, I would be a household word — and not just all over America, either, but also apparently in parts of Canada.

Curiously, this promise turned out, as a matter of fact, to be all too true. But Mr. Panitt did not tell me that the household word I would be would not be one allowed on a family show. I myself had to find this out, among other ways, from the thousands of letters *TV Guide* readers sent to me, my favorites among these being used in my last column of each reviewing season. These letters were hardly calculated to give one a superiority complex, to wit — and I will warn you, you will have to look hard to find any of that — the following:

Why doesn't Cleveland Amory go out and get a regular job? These days they can train almost anybody.

Another letter stated:

You put Cleveland Amory on the next to last page of your magazine. Why don't you put him two more pages back?

But perhaps my favorite was this one:

I think it is a shame that you have someone like Cleveland Amory to review TV stories. This man hardly ever has anything nice to say. Everyone has their own tatse, but this man has no tatse whatever.

TV Guide did not want me to use that letter in my column. The editors were very sensitive about misspellings or misuses of words in their letters, because they did not want their readers — particularly their advertisers — to think that only children read their magazine. Instead, they wanted me to use only letters which sounded as if they had been written by not only grownups, but intelligent, erudite grownups at that. I was often told, for example, that Henry Kissinger regularly read *TV Guide* — so many times, indeed, that I always meant to ask Mr. Kissinger if it was true. But each time when I was all ready to ask him, there was something about how he looked that stopped me from doing so. In any case, I could not run that particular letter above in my column — I had to respell "tatse." It hurt me very much, especially when I received another letter which went as follows:

You have a taste that is worse than Mary's, the girl that lives down the street from me.

The fact was that a truly extraordinary number of letters both had mistakes and were on the personal side, an example being the following:

Journalists like you, who distract the truth, are the ones Mr. Agnew refers to.

That one, at least, was signed, "One of the Silent Majority." By far the noisy majority of letters, however, were unsigned. So was perhaps my all-time favorite:

If "Dirty Sally" goes off the air, I personally will try to get you sued for defamation of character. It's people like you who cause so much child delinquency. . . . What are you, some kind of sex enjoyer?

Finally, there was another letter back to the magazine:

There is one thing I would very much like to know. Does Cleveland Amory have a degree in criticism?

That one I did answer. Yes, I replied, a Doctorer of Letters. Besides the letters, however, there was one wire which deserves to be included. It came from Sidney Sheldon, at that time producer of a show called "Nancy." About this show I had written, "Except for the fact that the idea is embarrassing, the execution exasperating, the plot silly, the characters stark, and the writing either for or by children, it is a fine show."

Mr. Sheldon's wire was firm:

I CANNOT STAND PUSSYFOOTERS. DID YOU OR DID YOU NOT LIKE THE SHOW?

Now there, I say, was a producer to conjure with. No wonder he became a writer.

Looking back over my actual reviews during my fourteen years of reviewing, I find that the ones which stand out in my mind stand out not so much for the reviews themselves but for what personally happened to me after writing them. The first was a show called "The Survivors," which began as follows:

> This show is entitled "The Survivors," and with it they should supply a kit. ABC-TV, who hired Mr. Harold Robbins in the first place, got what they deserved — a circumstance which could easily have been avoided if they had been able to persuade someone to read them one of Mr. Robbins' books. Mr. Robbins is a writer only in the sense that a woodpecker is a carpenter. Somewhere along the line he may, by the law of averages, have had an idea. If so the very idea of his having one was apparently so exciting to ABC that they forgot where they put it. In any case, it is not in this show. Our guess is the idea was to show Mr. Robbins' idea of the so-called "in" people. What comes across, unfortunately, is a good deal closer to the "in" people's idea of Mr. Robbins — the show is unbelievable and it is crude. When it isn't trite it's untrue — when it isn't sophomoric, it is soporific. Every character is a caricature, every situation is a cliche. As for the dialogue, it is to die. In fact it is our theory that one of the characters did die of it. On top of it all, the whole thing is endlessly moralizing — which, in a show as tasteless as this one, is the last straw. Somehow the idea of taking one's morals from Mr. Robbins is like taking higher economics from Bonnie and Clyde.

Just after that review appeared I was on Irv Kupcinet's TV show in Chicago, which featured a roundtable of guests. As I took my seat, I looked at my fellow guests and saw, to my amazement, one was none other than Mr. Harold Robbins himself. To say he was just as amazed when he looked and saw me is to put it too mildly. One thing was certain — I learned that for a critic to be a guest on a talk show and to be seated just one person removed from another guest he has said is a writer only in the sense that a woodpecker is a carpenter certainly did not make for airy persiflage. Still another thing was that, pointed as Mr. Robbins' comments were in my direction, they did not go beyond that. Actually, I have always felt that the reason they did not go further was that the man between us, our host Mr. Kupcinet, was, among other distinctions, an ex–professional football player. And, as such, he was used to observing ground rules and foul lines, and on his show at least, was clearly prepared to demand that his guests do the same.

The second review, the aftermath of which I also recall, was of a show called "Playboy After Dark." From it I excerpt the following:

The Playboy empire got its start by selling not only the American public but also Madison Avenue on the idea that pornography wasn't pornography as long as the editors put to press each month, along with their naked girls, at least a couple of respectable authors. From there on, the empire branched out into a chain of clubs — which equally cleverly sold the American traveling salesman on the idea that the farmer's daughter looked so well when dressed like a trussed rabbit that even if you couldn't touch her, you were a terrific big shot just being there and kidding about her.

From time to time, however, the empire also attempted

television, and here, alas, the success attendant on its previous endeavors has not been forthcoming. Perhaps television is less easy to kid. . . .

The interviews conducted by Hugh Hefner, the host, must be heard to be believed — and since he smokes a pipe and inhales most of his words, they just barely can be. Mr. Hefner, who is obviously amiable enough in person, has a television personality which can perhaps best be described as midway between technical difficulties and a station break. His conversation varies from dead silence to nervous *non sequiturs,* and it does not matter who he is interviewing — Mort Sahl, Melvin Belli, Gore Vidal — you have never heard them worse. On one show, the guest star was Don Rickles. Right from the start, he was unmerciful to Mr. Hefner. "Where," he asked, "is the dummy with the pipe?" Finally Mr. Hefner was pointed out. "Ah," said Rickles, "Charley Personality." Late in the show, Rickles was still at it. "Do you want to say something, Hugh," he asked, "or do you just want to sit there and smoke your pipe until morning?" Replied Mr. Hefner, "I'm just relaxing." "Well," said Rickles, "then don't have a show. Just go on the Titanic and watch the waves rise."

Once again the follow-up was better than the review. I had been privileged to go through the Hefner Playboy mansion in Chicago — a feature of which was a ground-floor bar over which, on the floor directly above, was a swimming pool with a glass bottom in which the Playboy girls disported themselves. In the middle of sitting at this bar, in the late afternoon, I was told that there would be a dinner party that night and would I like to attend? I asked the man who had invited me, the publicity director of the mansion, if they would be dressing. Apparently extremely sensitive on this subject, he immediately took offense. "Of course they'll be dressing," he said firmly. "They'll be dressed real nice."

The third review I chose was, again, less because of the review itself — because it was only one of a seemingly endless number of game shows I had to review — than it was because what happened afterward was something I have never forgotten. In any case, the review began as follows:

There are several ways you can avoid this show. But you've got to be nimble, because "Let's Make a Deal" has already been on two networks — NBC for four years and now ABC — and it comes at you both day and night. We have, incidentally, heard that the daytime version is worse. That is, however, hearsay. Having survived the evening show, we have no wish to press our luck. In any case, you have to stay alert and look at your TV listings carefully. Watching, that is, not *for* it, but *out* for it. For yourself, our suggestion is to lock your set, remove all connecting wires, leave your home, keep moving and do not talk to strangers. For your loved ones, who are perhaps trapped in your home, you should take all reasonable precautions. These would include the framing of this review on, or immediately adjacent to, the disarmed set.

We wish to be perfectly fair. This is not the worst show in the history of television. . . . Nor is there absolutely nothing which can be said for it. It is, for example, nonviolent — at least the show itself is. Steady viewers of it, on the other hand, are something else again. They should be paroled carefully and never in a group. Above all else, it is not like other programs, which are interrupted by commercials. In this one, you have commercials interrupted by more commercials. All the prizes are commercial and all the guessing involves commercials; as for the contestants, when they are not taking part in commercials, they do their best to be equally irritating. In fairness, this is not all their fault. Obviously they are selected for their U.Q., or Uninhibited Quotient. They dress in Halloween costumes, and whether they have made a good deal or lost one, they bounce about, giggling, simpering, squirming and, above all, squealing, in a way that can only be described as a poisonous combination of the last stages of TV ague and St. Vitus dance.

The immoderator of all this is Mr. Monty Hall. No other man living and few dead could put up with what he does and still look as if he's enjoying it. Our theory is that it's because he is not looking at it. He's *on* it, and *we're* the ones watching it. Then too he's a card with his ad libs. One contestant was named Janice Hertell. "Do tell, Janice Hertell," he said. Another couple was nervous. "You're shivering and shaking," he said. "No, you're Ronnie and Sharon." And sure enough, they were. Hall, you're a ball.

This time, after the review's appearance, I was in Los Angeles and went to a hockey game during which, at the conclusion of the first period, I went up the aisle to get something to eat. In the concession area I was suddenly accosted by Mr. Monty Hall himself. Without a single word of greeting, he whipped out a copy of the *TV Guide* with my review of his show in it and, with a sizable coterie already around him, and rapidly increasing in both size and anger, he proceeded in a loud voice, line by line, to read the review. Every so often he would pause to ask the people around him, by this time rapidly surrounding me, if there was a word of truth in what I had said — something which they obviously thought there was not — and who then proceeded, in louder and louder unison, and with more and more menace, to tell me so. Never before or since have I had such an experience with anything I have ever written, and I dearly hope not to. Not once during the entire episode did I ever say a single word to Mr. Hall, nor for that matter did he address a single word directly to me. However, when his group at last unsurrounded me I did ask one of them, apparently their leader, if I could go now. And when he seemed to agree, I felt it was my turn to close the agreement. It was a deal, I said wanly.

My fourth and final review I remember also for what happened afterward, albeit mercifully not so personal. The show was called "Queen for a Day." This time I feel free to favor you with my entire review:

> This show, which will shortly go into its 20th year, will soon have played to some 5,000,000 people — in the studio audience alone. Outside of the studio there are, apparently, still a few people who haven't seen it. In case you are one of them, it is, literally, miserable. It is a competition among housewives to see who can get to be Queen by telling the most miserable story — a dying husband, two or three dying children — that sort of thing, only keep it light, of course. Then, whoever

had the most miserable story gets to go to dinner at the best restaurant, the theater, nightclubbing and the rest. She also gets presents. One lady whose husband was out of work, and who had six children below the age of 5, received, for example, a lovely set of claret glasses. Needless to say, everybody cries with happiness. The Queen cries because she has won and the other candidates cry because they have lost — and the women in the audience cry because their sad story wasn't sad enough to get them up there where the real sadness is. Mr. Jack Bailey, who is pretty sad, too, tries to keep the crying down to a minimum with his rapier repartee. When a Mrs. Margaret Eleck, for example, started to cry because she wanted a bedroom suite because her house and chicken farm had burned down, Mr. Bailey quickly made her see the brighter side. "Ah," he said genially, "you're called Mrs. Eleck. Well, I'm often called that, too. 'Smart' Eleck."

All in all, it's a bawl. "It's the little things," Mr. Bailey says, "that really count with the ladies" — little things, we presume, like ermine capes, station wagons, deep freezers and trips to Africa. Some years ago one woman wanted passage so she could be a missionary. "What kind of missionary?" asked Jack. "Independent," snapped the woman. "I want to go into the interior of Nigeria where no one's heard of the Lord."

The woman meant well, we are sure. But even in the interior of Nigeria they had probably heard of this show — and not well. It is a star chamber of horrors. Commercial after commercial follows plug after plug. Nowadays, not content with a women's fashion show, they have a men's fashion show, too, full of more commercials — so that a Queen, who if she wins will be able to visit her dying husband, paralyzed by a spinal stroke on an ice floe at the North Pole, can also have the pleasure of knowing that she can take him a king-sized men's deodorant. On one recent show, another frustrated housewife wanted to be Queen because she wanted a new living room suite. She told us that her old one had been taken away by a man who had come to clean it and had taken it, and a $100 deposit, and had never come back. It had all happened on December 31st. "Happy New Year," shouted Jack. But somehow, after all the giving, we were all for the man. We think he had an idea for a brand-new show — a Take-Away, only keep it light, of course.

This time, as I said, I did not receive a personal reaction. Nonetheless, I remembered well that the show itself received, in addition to the minor honor of my review, the major honor of being chosen as the "Worst Program in TV History." This accolade was awarded by no less an authority on the subject than the actual producer of the show, Mr. Howard Blake. Indeed, a book about broadcasting entitled *American Broadcasting: A Sourcebook on the History of Radio and Television*, by Lawrence W. Lichty and Malachi C. Topping, includes an article entitled "An Apologia from the Man Who Produced the Worst TV Show in History," by Mr. Blake himself. "Sure," he wrote, " 'Queen' was vulgar and sleazy and filled with bathos and bad taste. That was why it was so successful: It was exactly what the general public wanted." Mr. Blake did not, however, tell us who it was who said that he did not know his bathos from his pathos.

* * *

There was one area of my job as a TV critic which, as far as I was concerned, cut close to the bone. This was the matter of animal shows. Over the years I reviewed everything from "Wild Kingdom" to "Me and the Chimp," from "Flipper" to "Lassie." But occasionally I would insert other nuggets of information where I thought they should appear as, for example, when I reviewed a show about an attempt, in a TV drama, to rescue a man on a mountain ledge. "Since the man was a hunter," I wrote, "I was cheering for the ledge."

It was not even much of a joke, and it did not make too much sense. Nonetheless, following the appearance of the review I received a call from the editor of the magazine *Field and Stream.* "That," the editor told me, "is the most despicable thing that has ever appeared in a national magazine." I told him I did not agree — that magazines had, after all, been published since the days of ancient Greece and even Egypt, and that surely sometime, somewhere, possibly in the very dim past, something equally "despicable" might have been allowed to slip by. I told him further that what it was, was a joke, and that if *Field and Stream* was all out of jokes perhaps I could persuade the Fund for Animals to lend them a couple.

At this the editor declared that he did not have to sit there and listen to that sort of thing, and that anyway it was not the first time I had written something despicable. "You once said," he continued, "that a hunter was caught in an avalanche, and that you were hoping for the avalanche." I admitted that he had me there — I had indeed so written. But I urged that he remember that avalanches and ledges were two very different things. There were, I told him, very few avalanches left these days — they were virtually an endangered species.

When I came to the job of reviewing a show called "The American Sportsman" I was at first undecided as to whether not to review it at all or to review it more than once. Actually, I ended doing it once and a half. This first half ran in March 1965, and went as follows:

> ABC has come up with a four-episode, hour-long se-ries covering the world of hunting and fishing and called "The American Sportsman." Here the narration is inept, the fishing is boring, the bird shooting pathetic, and the "he-man" exchanges embarrassing ("Look at those ever-lovin' birds! Hey man! Cock-a-baby!"). And every-thing they kill on those African safaris, of course, they're killing for the good of the poor, fear-maddened natives, all of whom are apparently refugees from the latest Joe Levine picture. In one sequence actor Robert Stack "bravely" shoots, at a distance of approximately one light-year, a feeble old lion who is billed as a "killer" ("The tribe will remember a man named Robert Stack — a friendly, capable man, an American sportsman"). In another, Joe Foss brings down, again a country mile away, an elderly, bewildered one-tusk elephant who is gently trotting along — and Foss, in turn, is billed as "standing in the way of the thundering, massive charge of a rogue elephant." In one show we heard the "Sports-man" defined as "the certain sense of good in each of us." Honestly, Sport, that's what the man said.

My second review was two years later — by which time *bona fide* celebrities were beginning to show marked reluctance to appear on the program. In any case, a part of this review read as follows:

Out of regard for their families, we will not mention the names of anyone connected with this show. Suffice it to say, however, that we have as host a man whose idea of communicating excitement seems to be to express even the most obvious explanatory remarks in a tone previously reserved for the deaths of heads of state. Along with him each week we have a curious assortment of white hunters in living color, about all of whose fearless exploits we hear *ad nauseam* — particularly as, armed with a full arsenal of weapons, they boldly advance to test wits and match virility with, say, a mourning dove. We also have guest "stars," a preponderance of them non-entities, each of whom apparently has to be identified as a "television personality" because otherwise you wouldn't know he had one, let alone is one. To top it off, as they approach their victims, they invariably speak in such school-girlish stage whispers that the only thing missing is for a house mother to shout "lights out!"

From the time the show first went on the air, animal people had, of course, turned on it in fury. By the time of that review, they were not only writing letters to the network, as well as to the sponsors and the host, but also to the "guests" who shot the animals. One of these guests, the actor Cliff Robertson, received so many letters after shooting another supposedly "rogue" elephant that, "in expiation," he told me, he produced, partly at his own expense, and also appeared in, a pro-elephant special called "Elephant Country." The late Bing Crosby, who, at the beginning of the show, whatever program he was on always seemed to be talking or wisecracking about "The American Sportsman" and promoting it, soon practically disowned the show altogether — for all his previous promotion. "I never hunt anything except birds," he told me, "I just don't believe in it."

Faced with such curious defections, and many more among other celebrities, hunters redoubled their efforts and desperately attempted to bolster "American Sportsman" with cables and letters. It was no use. First, Eastman Kodak dropped its sponsorship of the show after an advertising executive admitted that his company never should have been part of it in the first place, and, perhaps even more important, after admitting that there seldom was a slogan better designed for a company than the non-hunters' slogan for Kodak, "Hunt with a Camera Instead of a Gun." Then the program's other sponsor, Chevrolet, having also received an extraordinary number of complaints, also dropped the show. In the final analysis there were just too many people out there who were too angry — and, at long last, in 1971 "The American Sportsman" had a change in policy. No longer would the hunting of big game be featured — instead, rescue and relocation would be the keynote of all "game" segments. The hunters had lost. Again, in the final analysis, the fact was that their numbers had been exaggerated by everybody — by the network, by the sponsors, and even by the "guests." They could not keep on the air even one program, and that one on only ten times a year, on Sundays, in "ghetto" time.

Despite all this, I could not help ending up with a certain grudging admiration for one of "American Sportsman" 's stalwarts, Robert Stack. I followed his attempt to shoot "bravely," as I had put it, "at a distance of one light-year a feeble old lion" with several examples of his acting work on other programs. After another of these unfavorable reviews he demonstrated what seemed to me, particularly for a hunter, rare class. "Thanks," he wrote me, "for your continued support."

Before the horrors of the old "Sportsman" have been laid to rest, however, one story about it deserves to be remembered. It came to me from Sid Brooks, a writer who did two "Sportsman" shows. The one I remember best was supposedly the story of a "true" tiger hunt in India, with the Maharajah of Bundi. The "television personality" was Craig Stevens.

One of the Maharajah's men located the tiger to be used on the show for the final kill. The tiger was asleep in a cave. The Maharajah's man put a flag on the cave to mark it. A few hundred yards away there was a concrete structure which Brooks promptly named "The Bunker Hill Monument." This had been constructed near the turn of the century by the Maharajah's grandfather. Complete with thick concrete walls, it had slits or small windows from which, safely inside, the hunters could shoot. The Maharajah himself had hired half a hundred "beaters" who were paid the equivalent of thirty cents a day. Equipped with old muskets and tin cans to make noise, they had as their first job to wake the tiger.

Finally, the tiger did wake up and, bewildered, came, yawning, out of the cave. At first he started to move slowly up the hill, then faster and faster as he was spurred on by the shots, shouts, and tin-can banging of the beaters. He headed in the general direction of the bunker, but one of the Maharajah's trained marksmen actually "steered" him — by firing bullets all around him, one of which actually grazed him — directly to the bunker. In this bunker, peering out of the slits, were the Maharajah and Mr. Stevens. There were cameras in there too, behind them, looking over their shoulders. So, while it seemed as if the tiger was actually coming at them, with no bunker at all, the fact was they were, inside, completely safe. When the tiger, frantic to escape, leaped up, Mr. Stevens shot him.

That was what really happened. But, of course, for the program it was just the beginning. They had to go back and "re-create" — as they called it — to make the whole thing look dangerous. First they returned to the Maharajah's palace. Here the Indians had constructed, right on the palace grounds and especially for the show, a *machan* — a leafy tree platform from which, in the jungle, animals are shot. The Maharajah and Mr. Stevens climbed up on it and were told to have a conversation as if they were hunting together for the first time. Mr. Stevens was directed to whisper to the Maharajah as if there were a tiger in the vicinity. His script called for him to say something about being nervous. "Quiet, Mr. Stevens," the Maharajah whispered. "The tiger has ears."

After this, the crew took film of Mr. Stevens shooting, his rifle pointed at nothing at all. This "shooting" was then, of course, spliced in with the actual shots of the tiger leaping in front of the bunker. The impression the television viewer had was that the Maharajah and Mr. Stevens were sitting in a flimsy, open observation post with a fierce tiger attacking them — whereas in reality, the Maharajah and Mr. Stevens were on the *machan* and there was no tiger anywhere around. When they had actually faced the tiger, they had done so from behind thick concrete. In fact, the wildest animals around the Maharajah's estate were peacocks.

No less remarkable was the aftermath to this "true hunt." It occurred when Mr. Brooks and Mr. Stevens were present at the final screening of the show in New York. After seeing it, Stevens turned to Brooks. "That," he said, was the scariest moment of my life." To this day, Brooks does not think Stevens was joking — he thinks rather that Stevens, by that time, actually believed he had really been in danger.

Generally speaking, TV news shows have, over the years, been relatively fair to animal causes. A notable exception to this, however, occurred as recently as the early Spring of 1993 on, of all places, the long-time number one network news show, "60 Minutes." On the Mike Wallace segment of the show, Mr. Wallace went out of his way to defend a highly controversial experimenter who, at Louisiana State University, had shot some seven hundred cats in the head. The idea, ostensibly, was to learn how to treat human head wounds in combat. Although the cats were anesthetized long enough to be shot, virtually no painkillers were given to those who survived, some in excruciating agony, and the whole thing was so obviously cruel that it caused a furor all over the country. It was also extremely controversial scientifically — indeed, one of the so-called "discoveries" the experimenter claimed he had made had actually been made, and published, as far back as 1894. In any case the experimentation, after an investigation by the General Accounting Office, was ordered stopped by the Department of Defense.

All in all, it is difficult to understand why "60 Minutes"

would have resurrected the subject to begin with, unless they had somehow been persuaded to attack critics of animal experimentation. In any case, they certainly left no holds barred. I have myself known Mr. Wallace for some forty years — indeed, as far back as that I used to do a half-hour show with him on the old Dumont network — and had never known him to do such an outrageously lopsided report. What he did, in a word, was first to launch a merciless attack on a pro-animal young woman who could not remember if she had personally heard, or just read about, the cats screaming, second to give hardly more than a minute of time to the one doctor on the program who was knowledgeable about the cruelty, Neal Barnard, and then, third and finally, to give fawning praise not only to the experimenter but also to an American Medical Association spokesperson who castigated the whole animal movement.

A far better critic than I, Howard Rosenberg, of the *Los Angeles Times*, first extolled the virtues of "60 Minutes" in general, and then went on to point out that the show could also be, as he put it, "one of the shiftiest when it comes to tailoring a story to a particular point of view." Among other things, Mr. Rosenberg took Mr. Wallace to task for not once, but twice, misquoting what Mr. Wallace called "a tenet of many in the animal rights movement," that "a rat is a cat is a dog is a pig is a boy." The actual quote was from Ingrid Newkirk, who said that "when it comes to feelings like pain, hunger, and thirst, a rat is a cat is a dog is a pig is a boy." "The difference," Mr. Rosenberg stated, "is more than subtle."

Two weeks after the broadcast, when Leslie Stahl did the mail section of the "60 Minutes" program, she admitted that an extraordinary number of letters had come in about the cat experiment segment — apparently the first time Ms. Stahl had ever realized cats were popular animals. She then said that the same program had aired a segment on the miseries of women in India, and wondered why there had been so many complaints about the cat segment and so few about the Indian women.

It was at least one time when I dearly wished I had been still writing reviews. If I had, I would have tried to explain to Ms. Stahl that, where pain, hunger, and thirst are concerned, a rat is a cat is a dog is a pig is a boy is a woman is an Indian woman is even an American woman TV commentator.

CHAPTER SIX

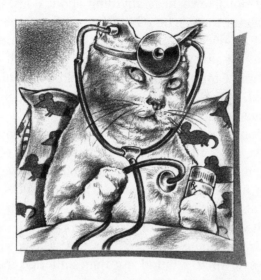

The Miracles of Modern Medicine — and Some Exceptions to Same

If Polar Bear was not around to save me from the Windsors or the celebrities or even the job of being a critic, he was very much around for something else from which he could not save me either. This was, frankly, an age-old illness of man and cat — and it was, as you may have guessed, arthritis.

Actually Polar Bear and I got arthritis at about the same time. I made clear to him that cats very rarely got arthritis — that dogs did, and that dogs also got things like hip dysplasia — but it did not make any difference to him. He did not like to hear anything about dogs, even bad news about them. The plain fact was he started limping around all over the place — just like me — and not the way he had always done, leaping on things and jumping. For a time I thought he was just making fun of the way I moved, but as time went by I began to see that he really did have a kind of arthritis.

Of course it was not anything like as serious as my arthritis. After all, I had a very important case of arthritis in both hips. But, just the same, he really did have arthritis, even if it was just a little case. Once I could see that, I could also see, all things considered — which I always do — it was necessary for me to repair to books about cat arthritis and find out more about it. And that is just what I did. And there I found out that, although the disease was, as I had already learned, and already told you, relatively uncommon in cats, when it did occur it was often associated, as one medical book put it, "with a variety of underlying problems." These the book went on to list as "congenital, metabolic, infectious, inflammatory, neoplastic."

Frankly, I always have problems with medical books when they begin to throw big words at me. Not that I do not understand those words, mind you, I just do not like to be bothered thinking about what they mean when I am reading something. Anyway, I put that book right down. But with one particular book I persevered. It was called *The New Natural Cat*, by Anitra Frazier with Norma Eckroate, and it had a whole section about cat arthritis. Part of this went as follows:

Arthritis is a subtle disease. At first, the little stiffness that creeps into the hips or lower back may not be recognized for what it is. "Well, he's not a kitten anymore," or "We can't expect her to jump up and catch the pipe cleaner the way she did when we first got her," may be all that is said to remark the subtle beginning of a downward spiral in the health of a beloved pet.

The disease is augmented by stress. Cats living under stress, such as those who are declawed or forced to live with incompatible humans or animals or those who are frequently caged, are more prone to the disease.

That immediately raised my eyebrow — I only have one I can raise. I was prepared to buy the idea that arthritis in cats could be made worse by living under stress. I knew it made my arthritis worse. I am constantly having to tell Marian, for example, to stop disagreeing with me about things because if she persisted in doing so it could easily make my arthritis worse. Anybody disagreeing with me, as a matter of fact, can set me off. I have found that when somebody disagrees with me in conversation, it is very much like when I eat something that disagrees with me. What happens when you eat something that disagrees with you? You get sick, that's what happens — which is, of course, where we get our word disagreeable.

But, to get back to the quotation from that book I mentioned, the idea of Polar Bear getting more stress and hence more arthritis because he had been declawed, was extremely irritating to me. I would never allow any cat I ever had anything to do with to be declawed. I regard it not only as cruel, but also as dangerous because it renders an outdoor cat virtually defenseless and even if your cat is, as he or she should be, inside, the fact remains that he or she may sometime get outside and then he or she would not have a chance against any dog or other animal.

Remember, please, I was not disagreeing with those authors because of the way stress in cats could be made worse. I was just irritated about this when it was translated to Polar Bear. Take another of their examples — being, as they put it, "frequently caged. Not only had Polar Bear not been "frequently caged," he had never, to my knowledge, been caged from the day I rescued him. He had, it is true, been put in a carrier on his way to the vet, and at the vet's he had, for one night, been caged — on the occasion of his having been neutered. But irritated as I am sure he was at the idea of being neutered, he could hardly have gotten arthritis from that.

That still left the matter of the third of the authors' three reasons — that stress makes a cat's arthritis worse when, as their book put it, cats are "forced to live with incompatible humans or animals." Indeed, where Polar Bear was concerned, I decided to take up the question of incompatible animals first, even though to do this I had to go all the way back to the days when I had brought into my apartment, hoping to have a companion for Polar Bear, a young cat which I described as the Kamikaze Kitten. The idea that Polar Bear could ever make friends with a kitten who bombed him day and night with sneak attacks, from as high an altitude as possible — the kitten's favorite take-off spot being the mantlepiece — turned out to be one of the worst ideas I ever had. All right, I admitted, it had been a terrible failure, but the whole aborted affair — which lasted, after all, only a few days before someone else adopted the kitten — could hardly have been responsible for making Polar Bear's arthritis worse if, for no other reason, because it took place a full twelve years before he ever had arthritis.

There remained only the question of his being "forced to live," as the authors of the book put it, "with incompatible humans." At first I refused to take this personally. I assumed what the authors must have had in mind were people to whom I had introduced Polar Bear. But even this, frankly, I considered, on the authors' part, exaggeration. After all, I did not introduce Polar Bear to just anyone.

As I began to think more about this, however, I realized that a casual observer, seeing some of the people to whom I introduced Polar Bear, might have jumped to the conclusion that those people were incompatible with him. Polar Bear did not, after all, cotton to strangers, and strangers were just what many of these people were. And often on such occasions, it is true, he would immediately go off into what I called his "put-off program." This would involve, to begin with, his pawing the ground in front of me, but looking in the other person's direction and, after that, sniffing the air, still directly in their direction, and then finally, looking squarely back at me, at the same time making very clear he was asking me when, for Pete's sake, was I going to do something about this person. Altogether it certainly was an attitude which, as I say, a casual observer might well have taken to indicate a certain amount of incompatibility. But this would hardly have been fair, because, though people were, to Polar Bear, certainly strangers, the fact remained he was that way to all strangers, both compatible and incompatible. In a word, where all new people were concerned, Polar Bear had already met everyone he wanted to meet. And, in all too many cases, the more they stayed around, the less he wanted them to.

Which left, finally, when you came right down to it, the possibility that the authors of that book meant that the one person who might be incompatible with Polar Bear was, if you please, me. Frankly, at first, I found this idea so preposterous that I had no intention of dignifying it by even mentioning it. I really doubted very much that those authors could, even in their wildest imaginings, have in mind someone as compatible as I am. Why, even under the pressure of some of the most tryingly unjust circumstances you could conjure up — which could easily cause a lesser person to lose his cool completely, and probably end up going off the deep end — I invariably remained the soul of compatibility. I sometimes, it is true, raise my voice at people who get in my way, or do not do something I want them to. But the plain fact is nowadays you have to raise your voice occasionally if you want to go on living.

Nonetheless, the more I thought about such a ridiculous idea, farfetched as it was, that I could personally be responsible for making Polar Bear's arthritis worse, the more I realized that it was up to me to attack the idea head-on and get rid of it once and for all. I even decided, on the remote off chance that a tiny bit of what those authors had the gall to suggest might have a grain of truth in it, to mend my ways, at least enough so that there could not be even a shadow of a doubt about my exemplary behavior. For one thing, I decided to keep my voice down — Polar Bear did not like loud voices from anyone, even me. For another, I decided to stop thinking about myself, and think only about him. It is not easy for me to think about other people, except about their faults, of which most of them have so many, but just the same I tried. Then too I focused on the arthritis question. I found my own arthritis hard enough to bear — the way, for example, it restricted my movements — but the more I thought about it, in my new unselfish way of thinking, the more I realized that to have such a disease inflicted on a cat, whose leaps, jumps, runs, and other acrobatics were, from kittenhood on, the very essence of his being, was ten times worse. In other words, I made the decision that as much as I would like to get over my arthritis, I wanted Polar Bear to get over his even more.

It would not, I discovered, be easy for either of us to get rid of arthritis. Arthritis, I learned from just about every book on the subject, even the medically self-serving ones, is hardly a disease which is any ornament to the miracles of modern medicine. The one thing you can say about it is that it is a disease from which very few people, and presumably even fewer animals, ever die, but once you have said that you have said just about everything. If people and animals do not die from it, neither do they ever get well — in fact, they get steadily worse, until they might as well die from it. I do not have statistics about how many animals have arthritis, but I do have statistics on how many people have it. These statistics say that close to forty million people in this country have at least one form of arthritis or another by the time they are in their fifties. By the time they are in their sixties, 80 percent of them have it, and by the time they get to my age I have no intention of telling you what percent have it any more than I have any intention of repeating to you how old I am. But I will tell you that, by my figuring, it is well over 100 percent.

To begin at the beginning, arthritis comes from the Greek roots *arthr-*, meaning joint, and *-itis*, meaning inflammation. And one thing that is certain about the disease is that, whether in man or beast, it is very old. It goes, indeed, even farther back from the Greeks to the Egyptians and, according to *Arthritis*, by Mike and Nancy Samuels, arthritis has been located in the fossil remains of a swimming reptile who lived 100 million years ago. When I first explained this to Polar Bear, however, he was not very impressed — he is not big on reptiles, whether swimming or not. He was not even impressed when I did my best to make clear to him that the very same kind of arthritis that he and I had — osteoarthritis — was found in Java Man, who lived half a million years ago. Frankly, I was not surprised he was not impressed at this — but one thing we both were sure of was that Java Man didn't get over it, either.

There are, of course, many kinds of arthritis. Some have arthritis of the hips, as Polar Bear and I did, and some have not osteoarthritis at all but rheumatoid arthritis. And, besides these arthritises, people arthritis, if not animal arthritis, can affect just about every conceivable joint, including those mentioned in the old song about everything being connected from the thigh bone to the hip bone or whatever it was. Indeed, arthritis runs the gamut from the neck, the shoulders, the arms, the hands, the wrists, the fingers, the legs, the knees, and even the toes. Indeed, Mike and Nancy Samuels add that secondary or traumatic arthritis can affect any joint that happens to get injured.

Just about the only good piece of news they had — and frankly about the only piece of good news I found about arthritis — was that it rarely affects the ankle. Immediately after I had found this out I carefully looked at Polar Bear's ankles and even went to the trouble of moving them around a little. He thought I was off my rocker, but the fact is he didn't seem to have a trace of arthritis in them.

Curiously enough gout, perhaps the most famous of all the arthritic diseases and the one which, in your granddaddy's day, was even then the recognized granddaddy of all arthritises, is perhaps the most extraordinary of all. The reason is that, while it does not involve the ankle, it does involve specifically the feet, or rather just one foot, and for that matter just one toe of one foot, the big toe. "Typically," one arthritis book tells us, "the initial gout attack affects a single joint — usually the big toe — and comes on suddenly, in the middle of the night." Unfortunately, the same book also tells us, "Little is known about what causes a gout attack to end, but all attacks are self-limiting and eventually go away by themselves."

Until they do go away by themselves, however, gout is incredibly miserable. I had an attack one night, and I really could not believe the pain — and all of it in one damned big toe. I tried everything. I tried wiggling the toe. I tried getting up and standing on the toe. I tried getting up on tiptoe. I tried just walking and moving around. But literally nothing did any good. The pain would vary in intensity, and it would come on and go off in waves. But just when you thought it was gone — or was at least really going — then it would come back again. I think Polar Bear thought I had gone completely around the bend, but there was one thing I was thankful for and that was that I had never read anything about cats getting gout. And, in Polar Bear's case, I was doubly thankful for this, because if there was one thing Polar Bear could not stand it was anyone messing with his toes. Even after fifteen years of cutting his toenails, when you would have thought he would have gotten used to it, he never did. Ever since he fixed one of his leery eyes at those clippers, he regarded it as the beginning of not just a brand-new war, but total war.

Although few arthritis pains compare to the pain of gout, the fact remains that in almost all forms of arthritis the pain never really goes away, as at least it does eventually in gout. But one thing is certain. Whatever form of arthritis you have, the chances are the pain will be enough to lead you, sooner or later, to try some of the most bizarre remedies known in the history of medicine.

There are, to begin with, a wide variety of venom remedies. That is right — that is what I said, venom remedies, and I am not kidding. Snake venom, for example, crops up again and again in books about arthritis remedies. And in case you are not happy about trying snake venom on your arthritis, what would you say to having a go at bee venom?

Again, I am not kidding. In one book on arthritis, called *Arthritis: What Works* — which by this time I expected to be a very small volume indeed — authors Dava Sobel and Arthur Klein reported on a couple who had even used bee venom on gout. Their report ran as follows:

"Bee venom cured the crippling arthritis in my toe joint immediately and completely," says a computer consultant from New Jersey. "My husband and I caught a few bees in a mayonnaise jar, and shook them gently 'til they were dizzy and vulnerable. Then we used long tweezers to hold them around the middle and placed them in the circle I had drawn in magic marker to show the area of pain in my foot. Bingo!"

My guess is that woman attended too many church socials. In any case, one thing I certainly did not like was the idea of treating bees like that. I know the woman said she and her husband only shook them gently, but still, keeping them in a mayonnaise jar and then using tweezers to hold them around the middle struck me as something of which I would not want to be a part — particularly when the bee gets just one sting a lifetime.

In any case, another report on bee venom stated that being stung accidentally was not the answer. This report came from a Charles Marz of Middlebury, Vermont, who stated that he had "provided free treatments with live bee stings for fifty years for the many people with arthritis who visit his home." Mr. Marz maintained that to achieve the desired result he had to administer to his patients, in the course of a year, as many as two or three thousand stings.

My feeling about this was that if the treatment did not sound any worse than having arthritis, neither did it sound a whole lot better. And, if there was one thing I was certain of, I would not try bee venom on Polar Bear. Polar Bear was not fond of bees. They made too much noise to suit him, and although, so far as I know, he had never been stung by one, he came awfully close to it one day on his balcony when he was sniffing away at one and I had to come to his rescue and explain to the bee that he should buzz off — an expression which, in view of the circumstances, I felt deserved no apology. I therefore gave it, and to my amazement the bee did what he was told.

Besides the venoms there are literally dozens, if not hundreds, of other curious remedies for arthritis. Many of these involve metals. Copper is easily the most favored of these metals, and people with arthritis have been wearing copper since the time of the Greeks. Indeed the wearing of copper bracelets, whereby some of the copper is supposedly absorbed through the skin to combat the disease, has not only long been touted, it is still highly touted today.

A friend of mine, Ed Kneedler, a fellow arthritis sufferer and a distinguished musical authority who now lives in Palm Springs, recently presented me with a bracelet, and I have worn it faithfully since the day he gave it to me, fearing that if I did not he would see me without it and be hurt. Actually, I have not found it has done me any good, but neither has it done me any harm — which, for an arthritis remedy, is really pretty exciting stuff, as witness the following report from an Arthritis Foundation Self-Help Course instructor from Indiana:

> Sure, I've tried copper bracelets. But other than "psychological relief" you only get green wrists. There's no harm in them, so if they make you "feel better" then it might be worth having green wrists.

I tried a copper bracelet — or rather, copper necklace — on Polar Bear and, finally, after much fussing — both on my part, for trying to get it the right size, and on his, on general principles — I got him to wear it. I watched carefully, however, to see that he did not turn green. If there was one thing I did not need, it was a beautiful white cat with lovely green eyes who turned all green. Fortunately, he never did. Neither, however, did his necklace seem to do him any more good than my bracelet did me.

If copper doesn't do the trick, arthritis sufferers can always take a more expensive step and go for the gold. "Gold," *Arthritis: What Works* tells us in no uncertain terms, "was first used to treat arthritis for the wrong reasons — when the disease was thought to be a chronic infection of the joints." Nonetheless, gold in either injection or pill form did itself proud in an arthritis survey conducted by the authors:

> Several of our participants used gold successfully for long periods of time — 10, 20, or even 30 years — before it finally lost its effectiveness for them. They never developed any side effects, they just woke up one day to find that the treatment didn't work anymore and it was time to try something else. Others got good results for several years before a toxic reaction ended the therapy. "Gold did the best," claims a housewife from Michigan, "but I developed a rash and got ulcers in my mouth. Now I'm on oral gold."

Even the metal uranium figures in arthritic remedies. I noticed it first in the almost endless advice one receives about travelling for arthritis. The best place to go, most books will tell you, is a hot, dry climate — i.e., a desert. But one book claimed the ideally perfect place for an arthritis sufferer to go was to an abandoned uranium mine.

This was perhaps the easiest of the arthritis remedies for me to abandon. I always think of mines, even in hot, dry climates, as cold and damp, and I just could not see Polar Bear and me grubstaking our way West, until we finally put down our stakes in an abandoned uranium mine — only to learn, when we had done all that, that it did not help our arthritis in the slightest. The only good thing I could think of about the whole venture was that, although we might be cold and damp and miserable for a long time, we sure would be in high cotton when the next uranium boom came along.

Curiously, not just patients but doctors, too, when they get arthritis, have resorted to going to extraordinary lengths when searching for a cure. Among these was none other than the world famous heart surgeon Dr. Christiaan Barnard, who travelled from South Africa to Switzerland for fetal lamb cell injections and then to New Zealand for green lipped mussels. Some doctors, too, have placed their hope in perhaps the oldest of all medical sciences — acupuncture. Developed thousands of years ago, acupuncture was discovered accidentally, according to one source, when ancient warriors hit by arrows felt instant relief from pain and illness which they apparently had for a long time before that particular battle. Although this discovery was not something I wanted to go to the bank on, the results favoring acupuncture in the Sobel-Klein survey for arthritis were higher than for any other treatment except gold. Even here, however, there were some dissenting voices. "Acupuncture," said one patient, "was great for my shoulders, but didn't do any good for my hands or feet."

Nonetheless, if acupuncture had its adherents, so too did just plain yoga. Indeed, yoga gave either temporary or lasting relief to thirty-six of forty-one participants, and only two had no relief. "If nothing else," wrote one yoga practitioner from South Dakota, "daily yoga keeps one *thinking* healthy and spry."

Besides the acupuncture and yoga believers, there are also a wide variety of food believers, not the least of whom are the fish oil adherents. Fish oil, taken in large amounts, produced promising results if one did not mind, as one patient noted, "burping up a fish oil taste."

Along with fish oil, there is literally a whole host of arthritis diets. The general idea of losing weight when you have arthritis, to make walking and generally getting around easier — if you are, well, less round — is of course obvious. But as for what specific foods and drinks are best and which are worse, lots of luck. I have personally read many arthritis books which, while generally agreeing on eating more vegetables, fish, and poultry and less meat and salt and fats, go on from there to be almost totally contradictory about specific foods. One book, for example, will tell you that dairy products should be avoided, while another will say that, for arthritis, milk is literally the perfect food. One book will tell you to eat as much fruit as possible, another will tell you to avoid fruit. One will say eat all the vegetables you want, another to eat some vegetables and avoid others. Even this they break down. One, for example, is pro-shade vegetables, another firmly anti-shade.

Along with diets, people with arthritis try an almost unbelievable number of different pills to relieve the day-to-day and particularly night-to-night pain of arthritis. People take aspirin, to name one, in huge doses — three or four five-grain tablets four to six times a day — often only cutting this dosage when, as the Samuels describe it, "Patients begin to experience ringing in their ears."

And aspirin is by no means the only favorite pill. There are literally hundreds of other pills which are taken to relieve arthritis pain. Unfortunately, an extraordinary number of these also have severe side effects. The particular pill I was given, for example, and had taken for years, ended by giving me the worst single ulcer pain, and indeed the worst ulcer I ever had. And as if this was not enough, shortly after I had stopped taking the pill I saw on the front page of the newspapers a story that the drug had just been found in tests to cause ulcers when taken for a five-month period or more. And I, as I say, had been taking it for years.

One of my favorite personal experiences with pills came from a man with whom I occasionally have breakfast at a nearby coffee shop. "You know what you ought to take for that arthritis?" he told me. No, I said wanly, having over the years suffered almost as much from the advice as to what I ought or ought not to do as I have from the disease itself. "Take alfalfa," he said sternly. Sir? I questioned, still pretty wan. "Alfalfa," he repeated. You mean hay? I asked gently. "Not just any hay," he said, "alfalfa hay. It'll do for you just what it does for the horses and the cows."

At last, I thought, I had at least found a possible remedy for Polar Bear. After all, if he was not a horse or a cow he was at least an animal, and an awful lot of animals eat hay. In any case, sure enough, in short order my friend showed up with a huge, wide bottle filled with pills and marked "Alfalfa." The pills were not small, either. I looked at the bottle nervously, still thinking of Polar Bear in size. How often do you take one? I asked. "One!" he exclaimed. "Not one! Take ten in the morning, and ten at night."

I took the bottle without a word. I could not summon the moral fiber to tell my friend I planned to try the pills on Polar Bear, but one look at those pills convinced me that there were few men living, and I presumed not too many dead, who could ever succeed in getting twenty of those monsters a day down Polar Bear, hay or no hay. What I did decide to do instead was to attempt to get just one pill down him. But to say this was a failure would be an understatement. It was a disaster. In the first place, the pill was too big for me to conceal it when I approached him with it. And, in the second place, it was so much bigger than his mouth that he assumed it was not a pill at all, but some kind of Frisbee. He was all for having a go at having a game with it, too, but he never did get so much as one taste of it inside him.

Unfortunately, I did not get any better from the alfalfa, either. But the reference to horses made by the man who gave the alfalfa to me brought to mind many examples of people who have tried various liniments for arthritis. Indeed, more than 70 percent of the participants in the arthritis survey said they used at least some kind of "Rub-on Balms." "Many of these products," the Sobel-Klein book declared, "are counter-irritants — that is, they try to make you forget about pain by irritating your skin to make it feel hot." Whether this is true or not, one thing was certain. Many of these "Rub-on Balms" had remarkably famous names, like Ben-Gay, and Sloan's Liniment, and Absorbine, Jr. "Ben-Gay and Sloan's Liniment are wonderful for me," a shipping clerk from California wrote in the survey. "If I take a scalding hot bath, cover my knees and ankles with liniment and wrap them in Ace bandages, I can sleep for a few hours with no discomfort." Encouraging as this was to hear, it was not my favorite in the entire survey. This came from a Georgia accountant — about the way he handled his arthritic discomfort. "I find," he wrote, "that making love *after* a hot bath or shower lessens the pain in my hip." It was good to think about, all right — feeling better without any medicine at all. I could see no reason why it might not be the start of a whole new field of sex science.

Not long after this I tried for myself a brand-new arthritis therapy — at least one new to me — which was written about in the *New York Times*. It was a biomagnetic treatment, and the idea was to bombard the affected joints with magnetic pulses. According to the *Times* article, the therapy had been first tried at a clinic in Waterbury, Connecticut, and now a new clinic had just opened in Melville, Long Island. Also according to the article, seventeen hundred patients had already received the therapy, and 70 percent of these had experienced at least some relief. Excitedly, I drove out to the clinic, although I did not take Polar Bear because I had already decided that if there was to be any bombardment, it had better be against me first and then, if it did any good, I could try it on him. In any case, during my first treatment, which lasted one hour, I lay in one of a long row of coffin-sized beds. If I was not comfortable, however, I did not feel anything from the bombardment of the pulses, which at least relieved my worry about the treatment. My relief was short-lived, however, because it was interrupted by the appearance of Marian. When she first saw me that day in that strange bed, she could not resist coming up and saying softly, albeit in a voice that could be heard by several other patients, "Rest in peace."

I went seventeen more times for the one-hour treatment, because the regime was supposed to be nine hours for each hip. And even after the last treatment, sadly enough, I did not feel any relief. Although I tried hard to maintain an open, if not optimistic, mind, in the end I had to admit, at least to myself, that I had not found that the treatment had to any major extent alleviated my pain.

In fairness to the biomagnetic people, the fact is that arthritis pain is an extremely tough customer. It is not surprising, therefore, that whole books have been written about this alone and, even in the books where all areas of arthritis are discussed, pain is given high prominence. In the book I have mentioned before, by Mike and Nancy Samuels, for example, there is a large listing called "Pain Control Interventions for Arthritis," and under this general heading there is one in particular called "Distraction." Under this are six separate items. The very first caught my eye: "Keep busy," it said, "with passionate interests, hobbies, work."

I certainly liked the sound of that one — at least all but the hobbies and the work. If there is one thing I can always keep busy with, it's passionate interests.

The Samuels' second recommendation was the longest one. "During painful activities," it said, "purposely think of something else that is positive (imagery), and/or mentally repeat positive affirmations (e.g., 'I can do it.')."

Frankly I am not big on repeating "I can do it" when I am not the one who is doing it in the first place. Nonetheless I was willing to give it a try, but I promise you I did it in such a low voice that no one could possibly hear me.

Suggestion number three was simple. "Listen to music, sing." That one I knew I would have no trouble with. In the shower, for example, I can really sing up a storm. Many times I have even gotten Polar Bear listening so closely that he actually got wet.

Fourth was even easier: "Watch television," it said. That one got to me. As I am sure you realized from having read the television chapter, I have heard of a lot of excuses for watching television, but being told to watch it to distract from the pain of arthritis did not seem to me to get the job done. Most of the time, far from distraction, what you would get would be the addition of having to see one of those awful new shows added to the pain of your arthritis.

Number five was perhaps the easiest of all. "Be around people," it said. That one I really jumped on with both feet. I have told you and told you writing is for hermits, and I hate it. It is much more fun to be around anybody, even somebody you cannot stand.

The final one suggested was right down my alley. "Get," it said, " a pet."

The only trouble with that one was what would I tell Polar Bear when he was in pain from *his* arthritis? I could not very well tell him to get a person — he already had one. But I certainly did applaud the idea of telling people to get a pet. One of my favorite animal soapbox speeches involves telling people that I believe in pets for senior citizens not only from the point of view of the increased adoptions for the pets but also from the actual therapeutic benefits for the senior citizens. The plain fact is that a senior citizen with a pet has to do what he or she should be doing for his or her own good — that is, to stop thinking about himself or herself. He or she simply cannot spend every waking moment worrying about his or her own aches and pains when he or she has a pet who needs watering and feeding, and just plain looking at and talking to, not to mention petting and patting, particularly when this is good for not only the pet, but also for the person.

In any case, for the difference in treating cat arthritis and human arthritis, I returned to the remarkable book *The New Natural Cat* by Anitra Frazier and Norma Eckroate. Readers with good memories will recall I have already mentioned this book earlier in this chapter. Readers with poor memories will not remember, of course, so they might as well go back and read that part again. Naturally this is going to keep all the rest of us waiting while they are doing this, so I will take this time to say that one of the things I like best about *The New Natural Cat* book is its subtitle: *A Complete Guide for Finicky Owners.* Everybody is always talking about how finicky their cats are, but they never talk about how finicky they are. And come to think of it, I honestly cannot remember the last time I met a cat owner who, when it came to finickiness, could not give his or her cat cards and spades.

Anyway, now that we are joined by our readers with poor memories, one of the most remarkable things about the book by Misses Frazier and Eckroate is their attention, when it comes to treating your cat for arthritis, to the matter of stress. Indeed, their very first suggestion about what to do when your cat has arthritis, right after "Consult veterinarian for a diagnosis," is "Check environment for stresses such as loud radios, careless children, and pollutants."

I went over these one by one. I never played a loud radio for Polar Bear — in fact, twenty-four hours a day I played for him a radio station which advertises itself as "Soft and Easy." No rock or any other terrible noises. Of course, the station still played a lot of modern music with lyrics which do not rhyme properly, but nowadays what can you expect? In any case, Polar Bear never complained about it and, like me, he was especially fond of Patsy Cline.

With the authors' second cause of cat stress — careless children — I am in wholehearted agreement. There are, in my opinion, three terrible ages of childhood — one to ten, ten to twenty, and twenty to thirty. And whatever age they are, there are very few of them who are not careless and nowadays, at least from my observation, are likely to remain so at least until they are thirty and perhaps longer.

As for the authors' third cause — pollutants — I am also an authority on these, as of course I am on most things. I am very careful, for example, about flowers. Flowers can be very dangerous for cats, in case you do not realize this. In Polar Bear's early days I gave them up completely, and in his later days, although we occasionally had flowers, I made sure to put them in high places well out of Polar Bear's reach.

Make no mistake, though. The authors of this book do not stop with radios and children and pollutants causing cats' stress. They also include grown-ups and partial grown-ups who have parties where, apparently, more people talk than listen. On this subject I agree with the authors completely. If there is anything I cannot stand it is somebody else talking when I want to talk. I know it upset Polar Bear, too, when I was talking to him about not doing something he was doing. Of course he went right on doing it, just as if I was not talking, but I still do not think he ever liked the talking, either. But it was not only talking the authors said gave cats stress. There was a whole list of other things. Their very first one, for example, brought me up short. It was, very simply, "Any surprise."

That certainly covered a multitude of sins for Polar Bear. For one thing, he put everything in the category of a surprise if he himself had not seen it happen before. For another thing, he also put everything in the category of a surprise if it was anything which had happened before whether he had seen it or not. But the authors of *The New Natural Cat* wisely confined their advice to, and I quote, "Announcing your intentions before doing anything — touching the cat, giving medication and so on."

In any case, the very next item the authors placed on their stress list was "Loud Noises." "Caution all visitors," the authors said, "to speak in calm and soothing tones." Sometimes, reading the book, I had the feeling that even the ancient Egyptians, who worshipped the cat, would not pass muster with these authors. But on the subject of stress they certainly knew what they were talking about.

Phil Maggitti, a friend of mine and a distinguished animal author, has, perhaps better than anyone, told the story of cat stress when it particularly pertains to outdoor cats — those without even the benefit of an enclosed wired run. The statistics, he points out, are inarguable — the life span of an average indoor cat is twelve to fifteen years, and that of an average outdoor cat at two to three years. Maggitti went on from there, in his typical humorous style, to number, backwards, his "16 Reasons Why Cats Should Be Kept Indoors":

16. They are less likely to be hit by a car when crossing the living room than they are when crossing the street.
15. Their owners are less apt to have rabies than are free-roaming animals.
14. Their owners are less likely to bite them than are free-roaming animals.
13. Their owners are not as liable to have fleas, fungus, or worms as are free-roaming animals.
12. It's unlikely their owner will transmit to them the Feline Leukemia Virus, Feline Immunodeficiency Virus, and other contagious diseases.
11. There is less chance of getting a leg caught in a steel-jawed trap.
10. When it's ten o'clock at night, their owners will always know where they are.
 9. Birds will like them better.
 8. Crotchety neighbors will like them better.
 7. They'll never come home looking like something the cat dragged in.
 6. It will be much more difficult for people to steal them.
 5. They won't disappear as often.
 4. Their owners will never have to bail them out of the local shelter.
 3. They sleep most of the time anyway.
 2. Their owners won't have to go calling them all

over the neighborhood when it's time for
dinner.
1. They'll live longer, happier lives, and so will
their owners.

In the middle of worrying about my arthritis and my
stress factors and Polar Bear's arthritis and his stress factors — not to mention indoor and outdoor cats and people
who claim the only way their cats can be happy is to be
outdoors — I had an accident. I was, in fact, hit by a truck.
Let me begin at the beginning. It all happened when I
was on my way to breakfast. Of all the things nowadays
which in my opinion are not what they were in the old
days I would put women first, and children second. But
I would put breakfast a strong third.

Start with your grapefruit — and before you even try
to start on it, ask yourself when was the last time you had
a really good grapefruit, a delicious, old-fashioned, sweet
grapefruit the kind which, when you were a child, was
everywhere. And if you do, by pure luck, manage to come
upon one, you can be sure it will not be possible to eat
it because it will not be properly cut. In the old days the
cutting of grapefruit was an art passed on from father to
son, from mother to daughter, among waiters and wait-
resses, busboys and buspersons, marmalade boys and marmalade girls. There was even a special spoon for grapefruit,
with one side of the spoon with teeth on it in case someone
had made a miscut and you had to correct it. Nowadays,
literally no one knows how to cut a grapefruit, and if they
do know they will not do it. It was so delicate, that fine
cut with a sharp knife not on the outer side of that delicate
inner peel, but right along the tender inside section of the

fruit. What you have today instead is something done by some idiot with a clumping machine which, I believe, was undoubtedly meant to be used for some outdoor purpose such as baling hay. In any case, that idiot clumps down three or four times on three or more sections of the fruit, and manages to render the whole thing totally inedible.

But enough about grapefruit. Polar Bear, like most cats, did not like fruit and so, when I gave up grapefruit, at least I was doing something of which Polar Bear approved. As for the rest of breakfast — and remember, breakfast was a meal Polar Bear and I particularly enjoyed eating together, he out of one side of my dish or plate and I out of my side. Or at least we started that way, and went on until his side was gone, and then he ate out of my side, too. But even Polar Bear, I believe, in his brief life noticed the decline and fall of breakfast.

One place he would particularly have noticed it, I believe, is at cereal. Look at your average cereal eater today, if you can bear to do it. I do not include children cereal eaters. Please do not look at them — it is too painful. They'll have milk all over their mouths. Polar Bear never had milk all over his mouth when he was eating cereal. But actually milk is one of the things I am talking about when it comes to cereal. Today I see person after person — forget the children — eating cereal, generally cold cereal by the way, with skim milk, that monstrous, blue, anemic, watery milk. In my day, in the good old days, what we had on our cereal was not anything like any kind of milk. There was not even such a thing as half-and-half in those days, either. What we had was good old-fashioned cream, so thick there were times when you had to spoon it out to get it. Of course we ate it on good old-fashioned hot cereal. A decent portion of that hot cereal, too, in a large bowl. None of these cold cereals in those awful little boxes that are so terrible to open — apparently on the theory children will get into them, and in any case boxes which, in case you haven't noticed lately, they are putting less and less cereal in.

All right, after the grapefruit and the cereal came the eggs. The eggs are still perfectly all right nowadays — the trouble is the way they are cooked. When was the last time, for example, you got a correctly timed three-minute boiled egg? You cannot remember, can you, because all you get today is a one-minute slurp of a boiled egg. Actually, I believe Polar Bear could always tell when a boiled egg was not cooked exactly three minutes and was, instead, just that one-minute slurp I mentioned. But that did not mean he liked it that way — he was just putting up with it, as I did, because he knew, too, that everywhere, but particularly at breakfast, we were constantly letting down, down, down.

In any case, forget boiled eggs and ask yourself whatever happened to good old shirred eggs. Today you cannot even find anybody who knows what a shirred egg was, let alone is, and if you do find somebody he or she will not know how to cook them properly. And if you do find somebody who knows what shirred eggs are, and even does know how to cook them properly — well, you are not out of the woods yet because the chances are that person does not know where to find a shirred egg dish. And let me tell you, a shirred egg without a shirred egg dish to cook it in and eat it off is not worthy to be called a shirred egg, let alone eaten as one.

Well, I will not go on. Of course, there were other things

which went with the eggs — kippers and herring, and smoked salmon, and cheeses, and marmalade, and all sorts of things. But there is no use thinking about it. Your old-fashioned breakfast has gone with the wind. My theory is it went that way because breakfast was a man's meal, and therefore was irritating to all the modern women who did not understand it. And let me tell you one more thing — the number of women you know who understand a good breakfast, let alone ever ate one, you can count on the fingers of one hand.

But no matter. Enough of breakfast, except to repeat that on the morning of the fateful day of my accident I was, as I told you, on my way to breakfast — I was going, as a matter of fact, to the New York Athletic Club. It is not a great breakfast at the New York Athletic Club, mind you, but it is a passable breakfast and that, for nowadays, is at least something. But as I say, enough of breakfast. In any case, to get where I was going I had to cross Seventh Avenue at Central Park South, and even as New York City crossings go this was a bad one. You get, for the particular light for that particular crossing — and in that time you are going straight across what amounts to three different streams of traffic — exactly thirteen seconds. First, there is the stream where the traffic from Central Park South goes downtown on Seventh Avenue. Then there is also a stream going the way I was going, east on Central Park South, across Seventh Avenue — but which sometimes decides to turn right to go down Seventh Avenue, and therefore can get you in the back. Third and finally, there is a stream going west on Central Park South which has an arrow which allows turning left to go down Seventh

Avenue. But the whole crosslight lasts, as I say, just thirteen seconds, and then the arrow comes on and the drivers who have been waiting for it have waited a long time, and are in a terrible hurry — particularly in morning rush hour — and they do not bother to be in one line, which they should be, but turn left in two lines. For these drivers, it is open season on anyone caught in the intersection.

That particular morning — at morning rush hour — there was not one but two trucks ready to make that turn left — one from the inside, or right, lane, and one from the outside, or wrong, lane. I had crossed more than three-quarters of the way as fast as I could, but I could not make it. The drivers of those two trucks appeared to me to gun their vehicles as if they were jumping off the starting gate to turn left and cross over that crosswalk as fast as they could. I knew, with my arthritis, I simply was not going to get all the way across, and that I was a goner. At the last moment I turned my head, and even considered that I might try to jump between the two trucks, but I was not up to that maneuver, either. All I can remember is raising my cane and shouting a futile "Stop!"

I do not remember a single other thing because whichever of the two trucks that hit me knocked me out, and the next thing I knew I was lying on the floor of a van. For a while I did not even really know this, but I at last learned it when I partly came to and noticed that someone who seemed to be sitting over me was wiping my face and neck — both of which were bleeding. The next thing I noticed, to my surprise, was that he was a policeman. And the thing I noticed after that — which was a pretty difficult thing not to notice — was that my neck was in a collar holding it to the floor. I asked the policeman if he could please loosen it a little. "No," he told me, "I'm not allowed to. I'm not even supposed to be wiping you the way I am." He then asked me, as he obviously had been for some time, if I knew where I was. I told him I knew then — that I was in some kind of a police car. He then asked me, and kept repeating this too, if I remembered what happened. I told him I thought I had been hit by a truck, and then asked him if this was true. He nodded, and then asked me if I remembered anything else. I told him I did not, but he kept on asking me anyway until finally I told him I did not want to answer any more questions, and why did he keep asking them? He told me he had to keep asking me questions so that I would not go back to sleep and perhaps lapse back into unconsciousness again — which, he said, would be dangerous.

Our conversation was not long, because I was being taken to Roosevelt Hospital, which was only three blocks from where I had been hit. I was also extremely lucky that the police were only two blocks away when they received the call about my being hit. For all the hurry to get me to Roosevelt Hospital, however, the thing I remember most about being there was what seemed to me, as I am sure most people experience at most hospitals, endless waiting. After a while, however, I saw Marian, and I was awfully glad to see her, despite the fact that just when she wanted to ask me about how I felt, they suddenly began what seemed an endless series of examinations and endless X-rays.

Actually the accident had been far tougher on Marian than on me because she had received just one message — which was that I had been hit by a truck and was being taken to Roosevelt Hospital. She had no idea of how serious the accident was. Typically, however, she got to the hospital almost as soon as I did and, awful as I looked, still bleeding, she was obviously relieved. "What hurts most?" she asked. My ribs, I said.

To this day I believe that no one who has not had broken ribs has any idea of how painful they are. It is not serious, they are not even bound as they were in the old days, and they get well by themselves without anything being done about them. But until they do get well, the pain is both constant and severe, and made worse by almost any movement. For at least a week I could not lie down in any kind of comfort, and at night I just sat up in a chair, doing everything I could to try to avoid any movement at all.

Actually, the injuries I received were described by the doctors in the emergency room at the hospital in one, what seemed to me, remarkable sentence:

Traumatic injury to body resulting in: fracture of the left lateral fifth, sixth, and seventh ribs, resulting in loculated pleural hematoma with contusions and hematomas to chest wall; closed head trauma, cerebral concussion with unconsciousness and post concussion syndrome; facial trauma resulting in contusions and large hematoma of the left forehead and left frontal region with swelling and large periorbital ecchymosis and hematoma of left eye extending to medial right eye, resulting in complete closure of the left eye with purulent conjunctival discharge; unsightly facial scarring and/or discoloration; contusion of the left hand; contusion above and lateral to the left eye with hematoma extending down left cheek to chin and neck.

One thing was certain. After a report like that, I knew that very few friends who asked me how I was would believe me if I answered fine, thank you. So I decided to answer in kind. I had to practice a few times, but finally I got it down pat. Once I get that loculated pleural hematoma under control, I said, and then lick that darned large periorbital ecchymosis, I will be fit as a fiddle.

In any case, when I finally got home I had various nurses of both the day and the night variety, but second only to Marian my best nurse was Polar Bear. He was both watchcat and guardcat. I have a wonderful picture of him, taken just a few days after the accident — he is perched on my chest, right up to my neck, glowering out at someone who was obviously approaching. Polar Bear did not mind walking up and down on my ribs himself — even though he soon figured out there was a problem there, and did it as gently as possible — but he was absolutely certain that he did not want anyone else messing around with me. Even Dr. Anthony Grieco, who looked after my arthritis and came to examine me the very first night, was in Polar Bear's eyes simply one more suspect. As for Dr. Grieco himself, normally extremely cheerful and optimistic, I could see he was very concerned, and I believe that somehow Polar Bear had picked up his vibes.

As for the night nurse, Polar Bear was actually very fond of her, and grew to regard her as, if not his equal, at least his relief guard. He stayed on the bed all day long and did not seem to sleep at all, but from the moment the night nurse appeared, although he stayed on the bed, he went almost immediately to sleep as if it was, then, all right to do so — his relief was on the job.

An extraordinary number of people who came to see

me had stories of people being hit by vehicles. I had never realized how often it happened, and the more stories I heard the more I realized how lucky I had been not to have been killed or at least hurt worse than I was. In many cases, I learned more about automobiles hitting people than I wanted to know. I learned, for example, that while, nationally, the people killed by automobiles are six times more likely to be drivers or passengers than they are pedestrians, in New York pedestrians make up half of all fatalities. On the non-fatal side, which I was lucky enough to be, the fact remains that nationally more than fifty thousand pedestrians are hit by automobiles every year. And although there are no figures on the numbers hit in New York in comparison to other cities, it is not too hard to imagine that New York leads all others by a wide margin.

With all the bad news I heard, I did, however, hear two stories I particularly liked. One was what Marian said to the lawyer working on my lawsuit about being hit. After he told her that money one might receive for an injury like mine would be tax-free, Marian's answer was immediate. "Don't tell Cleveland," she said firmly. "He'll do it again."

The second story was equally hard to forget. It came when I called Walter Anderson, my editor at *Parade,* and broke the news to him that I had been hit by a truck.

Walter was, as always, all heart. "How," he asked, "is the truck?"

L'Envoi

I remember well — as I am sure anyone who has ever been owned by a cat always does — the first time I knew that Polar Bear was seriously ill. I remember it well, as I am sure you remember when you knew your cat was seriously ill. It is like being stabbed.

For months, I had failed to recognize signs I should have recognized — but which I always attributed to his arthritis. For one, there was his increasingly poor movement of his front legs, let alone the continuing problem of his arthritic back legs. For another, there was the matter of his lying down in an obviously not-wholly-comfortable position and not doing anything to rectify it as he surely would have in happier days. For still another, there was the matter of the doorbell ringing. For some time I had noticed that when this happened, he would go more and more slowly to it. But now I noticed there were times, even now most times, when he did not go at all. Just the same, although I recognized all of these signs and many more I put them down, at least at first, when they were not so glaringly apparent, either to his arthritis or to his being not as young as he was. It was not hard to do — he was, after all, no longer a spring chicken, or rather I should say, as better befits a cat, a spring kitten.

But, as I said at the beginning, I remember distinctly the first time I recognized it was something far worse than either arthritis or the mere inevitable gradual encroachment of old age. I was playing chess with Ed Kunz, a Swiss gentleman and a close friend of mine who lives in the same apartment building. Polar Bear was, as usual, lying asleep beside me on my chair, and I was leaning over to pat him from time to time. But chess is a very absorbing game, and one time when I had not looked at him for some moments and reached out to pat him I suddenly realized he was not there. At almost the same moment — or at least so it seemed to me — I heard a thump. Polar Bear had fallen to the floor. Or, rather, what he had done was flop to the floor. Indeed, what I later reconstructed was that he had suddenly woken and then equally suddenly pulled his legs up from under him and then, as best he could, he had tried to jump to the floor. But, as I reconstructed, he had not really done that because he simply could not jump anymore. And by then, since his front legs were almost as bad as his back ones, he had just flopped — and had fallen right on his face.

It was such a sad and awful sight that for a moment both Ed and I could not believe it. I — who, in Polar Bear's heyday had seen him jump down from the mantlepiece with no trouble at all — was now seeing a cat who could not even let himself down from a rather low chair and, indeed, in trying to do so had stunned himself.

As quickly as I could, I reached down and scooped him up and hugged him, and made a big fuss over him, and then carefully put him back down on the floor, in his basket-bed. From that moment on, only when I was right with him and paying close attention to him did I ever put him on the chair beside me — and particularly not when I was playing chess. And never again did I ever put him up on a chair or sofa or anything else when he was alone.

The worst part of what had happened, both Ed and I knew, and spoke about it, was that the same thing must have happened before. Then too, and perhaps many other times, somehow he had gotten up on something when no one else was around — or someone had put him up on something, and then had forgotten about him, and had gone away. And those times, too, he had undoubtedly fallen just the way he had that time with us.

And also, of course, he had not remembered those falls. All in all, looking back on what had happened, it was not just sad and bad, it was also something which made frighteningly clear to me that not only is it awful that animals, when they are sick, cannot tell us or even try to show us what is wrong, they cannot even seem to be able to tell themselves — or at least, in a case such as that falling, to remember exactly what it is they cannot do anymore.

At the same time, something else was beginning to be very clear to me. This was that animals battle whatever infirmity or wound or disability they have with such bravery and lack of complaining that it must actually be seen to be believed. I would see that quality in Polar Bear many times that terrible Spring, and I shall never forget it. Every now and then I would hear one of his small "AEIOU's" — the sound with which I had grown so lovingly familiar — and the only difference I could notice now was that it was, a little eerily, cut short, until it sounded almost like a plain "OW." It was not, of course, but that is what it sounded like.

Anyone who has ever been in a similar position to mine, and who has seen his or her animal carry on a difficult fight, can only love and respect that animal more, particularly when you realize that it takes a very special kind of courage. It takes a courage which is very different from human courage but is, if anything, more worthy of admiration, because human courage comes at least armed with some knowledge, whereas animal courage often comes with no knowledge at all — not even, in the case of disease, knowledge of what it is they fight.

In any case, after that awful flop to the floor I knew it was high time, and probably past high time, for me to take Polar Bear to the vet. I had not taken him for some time largely because it has been my observation that most of the people I know either take their animals to the vet too much — for all too often a purely fancied ailment — or they take them not enough. Unfortunately, after first belonging to the former category, as I wrote in the first chapter I later belonged to the latter category. Also, besides now belonging to that "not-bothering-the-vet" fraternity of cat owners, I was also a member of that almost equally large fraternity of cat owners who have had at least one unforgettably bad experience at the vet's — and so have learned to dread a visit there almost as much as their cats do. These experiences, in the vast majority of cases, are very seldom ones in which the vet behaved badly, or even the owner did — rather, they are most likely to be ones in which their cat did. Yet these experiences, of course, reflect badly not only on the vet and the owner, but also on almost everyone within cat earshot or sightshot, except the cat. The latter, it goes without saying, could not be enjoying himself more — and the worse the experience for others, the more the enjoyment for him.

I did not, however, have such an experience with Polar Bear. I had it, however, with a previous Fund for Animals office cat who shall be nameless not only to spare his friends among the staff, but also to spare him or at least his memory. What he did, and did in fact more than once, was to use the vet's office as a battlefield on which to express his opinion of dogs. The most embarrassing of these forays was the day he chose as his opponent a truly elephantine mixture of an Irish wolfhound and mastiff. On this occasion, he jumped from his carrier not just at the monster, but literally over the monster, his desire apparently being to land on the top of the monster's head. He did not actually achieve this, but managed to land on the top of the dog's head and neck. From this position of advantage he proceeded to rain down blows, with his well-unclawed claws, upon the rest of the dog's head. During this period the dog, with remarkable restraint, merely shut his eyes and then did his best to remove the intruder, first by vigorously shaking his head and neck and then, when that failed, by trying to wipe him off with his paws.

In the end no harm was done, but when I finally got that cat back in his carrier, and clamped the lid shut, I realized I owed a wide variety of apologies to every person and animal in the room, not excepting the dog in question. To the latter, as a final fillip to my apologies, I released an affectionate pat. At this, for the first time the dog's owner spoke to me. "Don't you dare," she said, sharply, "touch my dog."

As I have said, Polar Bear was not like the cat in that story. He was, however, as are almost all cats, extremely wary of a vet office, and regarded it at best as somewhere between a Lebanon and an Iraq. Altogether, although he loved Susan Thompson, his longtime vet, he would not have been a cat if he was not glad of as long a time as possible between visits. But this time, since Dr. Thompson had moved away to Long Island, he was faced with Dr. Fred Tierney, someone who to him was a stranger albeit one who had long shared an office with Dr. Thompson. Although Dr. Tierney could not have been more gentle or more considerate, I could tell from his first examination of Polar Bear, he was concerned. When he finished, I knew from the look in his eye that the news was not good. And it certainly was not. What Polar Bear had was that dreaded age-old disease which afflicts, in their old age, so many animals — uremic poisoning, or kidney failure.

I cannot even now bring myself to go over the day after

day, week after week, step by steps Dr. Tierney tested and tried — the treatments which sometimes seemed to make him suddenly better and then, equally suddenly it seemed, failed, as well as those which seemed at first, and oh so slowly, to help a little and then, just as slowly, also seemed to fail. At home, I could tell he was going steadily downhill by, if nothing else, his failing to eat. Indeed, no matter how many different foods I tried and how many different ways I tried to entice him to eat, he hardly seemed to eat at all. And, as for his drinking, the only water I had managed to get down him was water I administered myself with an eyedropper.

I remember best, toward the end, the intravenous and subcutaneous infusions Dr. Tierney gave him. These infusions, which are basically a form of dialysis, at first seemed to help so much — and indeed sometimes lasted as long as to give him four good days. But then, in between the treatments, it would be three good days, and then just two. And, finally, the treatments would last — at least toward making him better — just one day. And finally, too, there came the day, just before the intravenous infusion, during which I always held him, when Dr. Tierney said quietly, "I am beginning to wonder whether we're doing the little fellow much of a favor."

I did not answer, but I knew the answer. Even Dr. Tierney's calling him a "little fellow" was a tip-off. Polar Bear was a big cat, but somehow his face, once so beautifully round and handsome, was pitifully pinched-looking, and indeed all of him seemed to have shrunk. I knew we had come to what I had allowed myself to think about as little as possible. From the very first visit with Dr. Tierney, I had hounded him with questions about how much pain did Polar Bear have. For if there was one thing about which I was determined, it was that Polar Bear should not suffer pain. I hate to see any animal in pain, but for the cat who had probably done as much as any single cat who ever lived for the cause of cats in general, and adoption of strays in particular, and had done so not only in this country but also in nineteen other countries where the books about him were published — for that cat to suffer pain was simply, to me, unconscionable.

Finally I came up with my answer to Dr. Tierney's question of whether we were doing Polar Bear a favor. I answered by asking him another question — which was, simply, how long could we expect to keep him going with the infusions? "I can keep him going for four or five weeks," Dr. Tierney said, again quietly, "but the last two or three will be very tough on him."

That, for me, was enough. Dr. Tierney and I made a simple agreement. We would see how that particular infusion did. But if it did nothing — as we suspected it would not — we would, the next day, let Polar Bear go.

The day was at least a day off, and so the next morning, when the infusion was obviously failing again, I sent for Polar Bear's close friends to come to say goodbye to him — among them every single one of the staff and volunteers from the Fund for Animals office. Each one of them held him in their lap, and hugged him, and each one of them, when he or she did so, was crying. As for Marian, she of course went with me on Polar Bear's last awful ride to the vet. Neither of us spoke a word.

Vets are not always keen on having the owners hold their animal or even being present in the same room when their animal is being put down, and the reason is that most of them have had experiences with it which do not make it practicable — experiences ranging from hysterics to last-minute changes of mind. In my case, I was pleased that Dr. Tierney never even mentioned it. He knew, without my saying it, that not only did I want to be in the room with Polar Bear, I wanted to be holding Polar Bear. Marian, too, had her hand on him.

The first injection was an anesthetic but then, before the final one, the sodium pentobarbital, something happened which I shall never forget. Polar Bear was lying on a metal-top table, and I was holding his head with both my hands and, as I say, Marian's hands were on him too but, just before the final injection, with what must have been for him, considering his condition, incredible effort, he pushed in a kind of swimming movement on the metal directly toward me. I knew he was trying to get to me, and although Dr. Tierney was already administering the fatal shot, I bent my face down to meet that last valiant effort of his, and with both my hands hugged him as hard as I could.

In what seemed just a few seconds it was all over. Dr. Tierney did a last check. "He's gone," he said quietly. Only then did I release my hugging hold, but, as I say, I still remember that last effort of his, and I shall remember it always. I only hope that someday I shall forget that part of my memory which tells me that I was part of doing something wrong to him, but rather there will remain only the memory that I was part of doing something which had to be done.

Actually, leaving the room, I was good — at least I was good leaving the examination room. When I got to the outer office, however, I saw Dorsey Smith, a dear friend of mine and Polar Bear's too, who was holding her own cat in her hands. "Is it Polar Bear?" she asked me. I nodded. But when she also asked, "Is he all right?" I could not even shake my head. Instead I did something so unknowingly, so un-Bostonian, and so un-Me — something I could not help, not even just in front of Dorsey, but with all those other patients there, too — I burst into tears. It was embarrassing, and I was ashamed, but the worst part was that, for the first time in my life that I can remember, I could not stop crying.

I wasn't too good afterwards, either. My daughter Gaea, who lives in Pittsburgh, had wanted to come to New York for a visit, although I knew she just said that so she could be with me when I lost Polar Bear. She had always been very fond of him. What she wanted to do that very afternoon, she said when I met her, was to go to see the movie *Howards End*. I knew that was something she had made up, too, because she did not want me to go back to the apartment until Marian had had a chance to remove Polar Bear's things, or at least hide them in a closet.

I played along with this deception, although I knew what was going on. I also knew I would not like *Howards End*, and I did not. Whoever Howard was, he certainly had no end and neither, it seemed, did his movie — although I doubt that I am being fair to it, because that particular afternoon I probably would have found fault with even one of my favorite movies, like *All About Eve* or *Double Indemnity*.

In any case, when Gaea and I got back to the apartment, Marian was there, and she had indeed done an excellent job of removing and hiding at least most of Polar Bear's things — the basket-bed, the toys, the scratching post, his dishes, and even his litter pan. Anyone who has had to go through an animal's death — and we all do sooner or later, and many times, too, in our lives — knows what it is like to come upon a favorite toy, a favorite ball of yarn, or indeed a favorite anything, or even something which was not a favorite, but which was still his or hers. Even a dish can do it. Although, as I say, Marian had removed all his regular dishes, I still came upon much later, when neither Marian nor Gaea were there, a little dish I liked to put his nightly snacks on. I took the dish, and sat down with it in my hand. I turned it over and over, and just sat there, and kept sitting there for so long I actually fell asleep with it. It made no sense, but then, at a time like that, more things do not make sense than do. It is the first part of the miserable loneliness which lies ahead for you, because what you are still trying to do, of course, whether you know it or not, is to hold on to your animal.

But even coming across one of your animal's things is not by any means all of what you must go through. You must also go through sitting and looking and listening, and actually thinking you see or hear your animal. At such a time, even a look at one of your animal's favorite places will be too much for you and, during the first few nights, if you are anything like me, you will not only see and hear your animal before you go to sleep — if indeed you can sleep — you will even feel his paws padding on your bed and then, after that, you will dream about him. My dreams were awful — Polar Bear in trouble, and in a place where I could see him but could not get to him — or else me in trouble, where he could see me but for some reason would not come to me. So many dreams had just one or the other of these two plots — so similar they seemed like endless replays.

But for me the worst part was not the sitting and thinking, or the lying and sleeping, or even the dreaming — it was the simple matter of coming home and not finding him at the door. Polar Bear always seemed to know from the time I stepped out of the elevator that it was me, and he would always be walking back and forth just out of reach of the door as it swung open, and yet near enough to rub against my leg. Whereupon, always, I gave him first a pat, then a pull-up, then a hug, and finally a hold-up of him over my head. It was our ritual.

Now, of course, there was nothing. No him, no rub, no pat, no pull-up, no hug, no hold-up, no nothing. Night after night I would come home and just walk in quickly and sit down, still in my coat. The whole apartment had, for me, become an empty nothingness. I can only describe it as living in a void. I did not want to be anywhere else, but neither did I really want to be there. It was not just that Polar Bear was not there — it was the awful, over-powering weight of knowing he was never ever going to be there again.

As I write about it all now, I realize something I did not realize then — how lucky I was compared to so many others who have to face the loss of their animal without other animal people around them. I, at least, was sur-rounded by animal people. There were calls and letters and cards and wires and even faxes. And they all were so completely understanding, because they had all ob-viously, at some time or another, been through it them-selves. I remember perhaps best a card from my friend

Ingrid Newkirk. "Damn them for dying so young," she wrote, in her inimitable inverse-perverse way. After reading that I laughed — the first real laugh I had had since Polar Bear died.

I compared, during this time, my good fortune in having such understanding friends as against the fortunes of those whose sadness, I knew, must often be greeted with such incredible lines as, "But after all, it was just an animal," or even, "Why don't you just get another?"

Of one thing I was certain. Anyone who ever said either one of those things to me would not be likely ever to say one of them again — at least not in my presence. In any case, during this period I made it my business to learn about the extraordinary number of books and pamphlets about animal loss there are nowadays, not to mention the hundreds of support groups and even hotlines to which those faced with the loss of an animal can turn. Up until the 1970's, I learned, there were almost none of these in existence. Now there is even a group called the Delta Society in Renton, Washington, which, on request, can supply not only a formidable listing of these groups, but also a wide variety of video and audio tapes. Their videos and tapes are fine, too, but somehow when I ordered mine, I was surprised to learn that I should allow up to four weeks for delivery, which seemed to me somewhat tardy for immediate grief sustenance.

Some of the pamphlets on the subject were extraordinarily detailed. One, from the Marin County Humane Society, was called "The Stages of Grief," and proceeded to list five of these. The first was called "Denial" ("Your first reaction to the news that your animal has died or is about to die — you simply do not want to believe it"). The second was "Anger" ("Why did my animal die? Why did you leave me when I needed you most?"). The third stage was "Bargaining" ("You promise to spend more time with your animal, to never forget his/her mealtime again, to shower your animal with gifts, if only he/she will stay with you a little longer"). The fourth was "Depression" ("A time when your tumultuous emotions ebb into one sorrowful expression, when most people feel a lack of motivation and would like to withdraw from the busy, happy world"). The fifth and final one was "Recovery" (one which, it was stated, "Allows you to take a fresh look at yourself and the world around you").

Frankly, I did not find any of those stages held much comfort for me in getting over my grief about Polar Bear. However, among Delta's videotapes I found one particularly helpful. It was about a grief support program at Colorado State University called *Changes*, and it was not authored by a veterinarian, as so many videotapes are, but by a non-professional. His name was Art Batchelder, and in the tape he tells the story of what happened to him when, after fourteen years, he lost his dog, a sheltie-terrier named Dusty — or at least what happened to him until he met a counselor at *Changes* named Carolyn Butler:

> Carolyn and I had a long talk. Carolyn told me that it's O.K. to cry. She told me that grieving isn't going to be over in a week or two or a month or a year. It may take two, three, several years. She was right.
>
> She told me something then I didn't quite understand or believe what she meant, but I know now was absolutely true. She said, "Art, when Dusty died, a part of you went with him." And yes, it did.

She helped me grieve. In my generation, we grew up with the John Wayne syndrome — men don't cry, men don't show emotions, we're macho, we're heroes. So I couldn't let myself cry in front of anybody. I told her, I drive around in that truck and Dusty's not there and I want to talk to him. She said, "Talk to him, Art."

I wanted the veterinarian to tell me the same thing that Carolyn did, that "Art, it's O.K. to cry. Grief is going to be very difficult — you're going to hurt, and you're going to hurt deeply. Don't hold it in. Talk to people. Let people know that you're hurting. Go talk to Dusty's picture, pick up that urn" — I didn't pick up that urn for two or three months, I didn't touch it. My daughter carried it home, I could not touch it.

And I think they've got to let the person know that it's O.K., that grief for a pet *is* acceptable, it *is* normal. I told the group one time that grieving for a pet is far worse than grieving for a human. And one woman said, "What do you mean by that, Art?" I think she was almost offended. What I meant was if you lose a brother or sister or a parent, it's tremendous grief, it's a tremendous loss, but you have a funeral, you have a memorial service, people come, you get cards, people talk to you. I could walk down the street later and somebody might come up and say, "Art, I'm so sorry to hear about your Dad. He was such a nice man," or something like that. Nobody ever came up to me as I was walking down the street and said, "Art, I'm so sorry to hear about Dusty. He was such a nice dog." Nobody ever came and told me they were sorry that I lost Dusty. . . .

I couldn't take my walks any longer because I couldn't walk along the streets where Dusty and I went. But then

I started taking the walks. I went out one Sunday morning — we had special routes we would take on different days of the week — and I went out one Sunday morning, and there were other people walking with their dogs and I said, I can't do this. I went home.

But after talking to Carolyn I went out there one Sunday morning and I walked, and I saw other people with their dogs, and there was a tug on this hand — I felt it — and I visualized Dusty down there. I'm not going to say Dusty was there, but I visualized Dusty there, and we walked down that street and the tears just flowed down my face, and people saw me, and I didn't care. Because I was proud I had that guy with me.

What Mr. Batchelder found helpful in getting over Dusty — talking to him and pretending he was there when he knew he was not — might not be the answer for everyone, but it obviously was helpful for him. It was also helpful for me, and particularly so, perhaps, in my case because Dusty was a dog and not a cat. In any case, I also found helpful a passage in a book entitled *Courage is a Three-Letter Word,* by Walter Anderson, in which he gave "Don'ts" and "Do's" about how to behave around someone who is grieving not for either a dog or a cat, but a person. The reason I found this passage so helpful was that, although Anderson had obviously written it about the passing of a person — in fact, his father — he told me he would not change it if it was for the passing of an animal. In any case, I found Walter's first two "Don'ts" particularly memorable:

*Don't pretend. Don't make believe you're there for some other reason; do not divert conversation to other, what

you consider "less painful" subjects. Survivors usually want to talk about their loss, so this should be encouraged.

Don't try to make the bereaved feel better. Although this may seem at first like a contradiction, it is not. I don't know how many funerals I've attended where well-meaning people have advised, "Don't take it so hard." It leaves the bereaved no response and encourages them to conceal their grief. The last time, which was the *last* time, I said, "Don't take it so hard," a survivor asked me, "How hard *should* I take it?"

Many times, going through the loss of Polar Bear, when someone said to me, "Don't take it so hard," I would indeed have liked to answer, as Mr. Anderson did, how hard *should* I take it?

Unlike some people who have experienced the loss of an animal, I did not believe, even for a moment, that I would never get another. This is not to say that I joined the people who said either "After all, it's just an animal," or "Why don't you just get another?" either in spirit or in any other way. But I did know full well there were just too many animals out there in need of homes for me to take what I have always regarded as the self-indulgent road of saying the heartbreak of the loss of an animal was too much ever to want to go through with it again. To me, such an admission brought up the far more powerful admission that all the wonderful times you had had with your animal were not worth the unhappiness at the end — and, regardless of what that meant for you, it meant for your animal that his or her life was meaningless. Nor could I take what seemed to me another self-indulgent road — that to get another animal would be too disloyal to your previous animal. To me, that argument seemed equally spurious as the unhappiness one, and for the same reason — that his or her life was, in the end, again, meaningless.

Like most people, however, I did not want to get another animal right away. To the kind of people who offered to go out and buy one for me, I was polite but firm. I told them that I appreciated their generosity, but there were far too many animals at shelters waiting, all too often hopelessly, for homes for me to consider buying one for myself, let alone letting them buy one for me.

Nonetheless, since I myself had brought up the subject of getting another animal at a shelter, I could not help but realize that this was something else again. And, as time passed, I found myself thinking more and more not just about how lonely my apartment was, but rather how nice it would be to have a friend on four paws around. My first choice was Polar Star, who, faithful readers of my second book about Polar Bear will recall, came to me via Anna Belle Washburn and the Martha's Vineyard Shelter. Polar Star was white, and looked very much like Polar Bear except that Polar Bear's eyes were green and Polar Star's were blue, and that Polar Bear had five toes on his front paws, and Polar Star had six. Like Polar Bear, Polar Star too had been a stray — incredibly enough, he had been purposely left behind when a family of no mean means, but certainly no other recommendation, had left him to fend for himself when they went back to the city after their summer vacation.

As I went through the Martha's Vineyard Shelter, Polar Star reached one of his six-toed paws out from one of the upper cages and patted me on the cheek as I started to go by — something I have always felt was a put-up job, carefully arranged by Anna Belle. But it certainly worked — from that moment I was a goner for Polar Star, and he soon became my second-favorite cat in the world — big, beautiful, bear-like, benevolent, and *bonhomous*. He would, however, I knew from the beginning, have to be one of the Fund for Animals' office cats, because Polar Bear was very sensitive about other cats being, first, within several miles of him and, second, within several more miles of me. Now that Polar Bear was gone, however, I would be free to take Polar Star to my apartment.

Or so I thought. I knew everybody in the office was crazy about Polar Star, but I thought their feeling for my loss of Polar Bear would overcome any selfish feeling they might have about parting with Polar Star. If so, I was, as so often one is now with any kind of help, rudely mistaken. To a man — and only one was a man — they drew the line at Polar Star going anywhere. Sean O'Gara was at least reasonable, but not so Lia Albo. Lia thought little of the idea of my taking Polar Star because she felt a cat she had foisted on us would also miss him. That cat, incidentally, was named Freddie, and though he was not named for my editor, Fredi, he well could have been because, although he is a male and my editor is a female, both are two parts panther and one part Bengal tiger. In any case, the strongest opposition to my taking Polar Star away was Amy Ballad, who was closer to the cat in question than anyone — and vice versa — and said nothing as forcefully as I have ever heard nothing said. Even Marian was of little use to me. In her opinion, Polar Star was the Fund for Animals' official greeter — he loved everybody, new people as well as people he already knew — and he belonged where he was.

I was not a happy camper, an expression I have never been fond of — possibly because I was not particularly happy when I was at camp. All of them, I pointed out, had forgotten that it was I, not them, to whom Polar Star had been given. All of them also, I added, had their own animals in their own apartments or homes, and I alone was in solitary confinement. Even this meaningful argument fell upon deaf ears. I could get, they felt, just as much enjoyment from Polar Star as they did, and why was that not enough for me when I could also perfectly well get another cat at home, and still enjoy Polar Star at the office? Infected as they all were — at least except for Marian — with the idea that all modern offices should be democratically run, I stood as much chance for a favorable vote on the issue as the late Herbert Hoover. Suffice it to say that arrayed against me was not only the New York office, but also the Washington office of the Fund for Animals which, as run by national director Wayne Pacelle, I am doing a favor to call democratic. Actually, it is one of the last places on earth in which you experience pure socialism.

Against such odds, in the end, ungraciously as ever, I gave in. At about the time I did so, however, Bo and Natalie Jarnstedt, noted animal rescuers and friends of the Fund, decided to have a party for animal people at their Greenwich, Connecticut, home. During this party Marian was invited by Natalie into a large bathroom in which were ensconced Natalie's latest rescuees. One of these was a tiny, tiger-striped orange tabby with large owl eyes which were purely golden — a kitten who had been born, Natalie informed Marian, in the Greenwich, Connecticut, town dump. The minute Marian laid eyes on the kitten she wanted me to see him and, when I did, I knew full well what Marian and Natalie had been plotting.

Actually, the kitten was as different from Polar Bear as could be — something which is one of my theories, that people looking to "replace" an animal they have lost should not think of looking for something similar. This all too often invites unfair comparisons. At the same time, I should admit that this kitten did have at least one of Polar Bear's prime characteristics. Even at his minuscule size, and at the age of less than a month, he was already incredibly brave. That very first time I saw him he was not only unfazed by, but actually holding his own against, two other larger cats and, on top of this, two dogs. His very bravery named him for me — he would never be anything but Tiger Bear. In any case, once more I was a goner, and in a remarkably short time I had a new cat, or rather, kitten.

The distinction is important. I had never had a kitten as my own animal before, and to say they are not the same as full-grown cats is an understatement. From the moment Tiger Bear arrived at the apartment it was close to impossible for anyone, even friends of mine who are not dedicated cat people, to take their eyes off him. He had already had many trips to the vet because of the difficulty of his early life at the dump, and he had many problems, like ear mites, and every kind of worm you could imagine. I knew from his background he would have many more problems, but you would never know to look at him he had a single one of them. His energy, his curiosity, his playfulness, and his spoiling-for-a-fight-fulness were all unbelievable. So was his extraordinary ability not only to leap impossible heights on straightaways, but also to seem to fly from one place to another. I have seen him do acrobatics which would shame a monkey, and the monkey, after all, has hands — and Tiger Bear would shame him with just his paws. He would leap, for example, from the floor to the top of the back of a tall chair, then come, with all four paws somehow on this perilous perch, see-sawing for a moment and land on the top of a tall bookcase. He would also start a run down the living room and literally bank off the back of one chair, onto another chair, and end up on the highest thing he could find. As for his chewing, please do not mention it. There is literally nothing in my apartment he has not tried to chew — from the telephone cord to my sorest finger.

While watching this extraordinary animal grow, I remembered that when he was born in that dump, for ten days he, like most kittens, could not open his eyes and had not, at that age, any sense of smell at all. In fact, the only sensory ability he had was to be able to hear his mother's purr — otherwise he would undoubtedly not have lived. Eventually, however, not only did he live but, such are the accomplishments of Natalie as a rescuer, eventually both his mother and father were also rescued.

Not the least curious thing about my new friend was learning that in his tiny little body he had two-hundred and thirty bones — twenty-four more than we humans have. He also had an unbelievably supple spine, one that can twist and turn and, helped by his tail as a rudder, could always manage a safe landing. I learned, however —

early and often — that there is no such thing as kitten-proofing the home. Wherever you most do not want your kitten to go, that is assuredly where he most dearly wishes to go, and where he will get by hook or by crook, and sometimes both. Scientists would have us believe that cats do not display either what they call "insight learning" or reasoning ability, and maintain that their learning is based entirely on experience. Based entirely on my experience with Tiger Bear the kitten — and remember, he was nowhere near to being a grown cat — he had all the insight learning I could handle, and then some. As for his reasoning ability, let me give the scientists just one example. There is one particular closet where I do not wish him to go except when I am around — there are too many things in there with which he could hurt himself. So, where in the whole apartment does he most want to go? You guessed it. Furthermore, he soon learned that even if he could not handle the closed doorknob, he found out that if he pulled just right on the tote bag which was hanging on the doorknob — not so far out that the bag came off the knob, but far enough so that pulling on it put pressure on the doorknob — he could get the closet open. "Insight learning" nothing — it was pure out-of-sight learning.

Tiger Bear's favorite sport is assassinating anything in the apartment which he regards as having to do with something which people do instead of paying attention to him. Prime among these targets are the chess board and the chess men. He likes best the ruckus it causes when he manages a single-paw assassination of an entire, and hitherto very close, game. But he is not adverse to the capture of single hostages — he prefers a king or a queen — which he imprisons in, and preferably under, as many difficult places as possible.

One of the things he has taken his time learning is saying even a remotely respectable meow. Polar Bear had his crystal-clear AEIOU, but Tiger Bear, either because he did not have enough cats around when he was growing up or for some other reason, makes sounds which do not seem even to be based on any other sound except one made by a not-very-well bird. They are strictly off-key, and off anything but dissonance. It does not bother me, however, because, for all the trouble he has been, for me he makes up for this a hundred times by his constant following of me wherever I go. I put it down to the fact that he must have had so little individual attention in his early life that he has grown very rapidly to be very dependent on it. All in all, when my friend Ogden Nash wrote that awful poem: "The trouble with a kitten is that / Eventually it becomes a cat," all he did was illustrate that he did not know the first thing about either cats or kittens. The fact is there is no trouble with a kitten. And, eventually, it becomes exactly what you always hoped it would.

Finally, there remains, to those who have lost an animal, two large questions. The first of these involves the matter of whether or not to bury your animal. I have always believed that, as I said in the introduction to this book, the best place to bury your animal is in your heart. I believe that fully. At the same time, since so many people knew Polar Bear, and wanted to know where he would be buried, I finally gave in. I chose as his final resting place

the Fund for Animals' Black Beauty Ranch which, over
the years, has become home to thousands of abused or
abandoned animals. To Chris Byrne, the able manager of
Black Beauty, as well as to his extraordinary wife, Mary,
fell the job of finding the right place, the right headstone,
and the right copper plaque. They did it all wonderfully
well. The plaque is not only a lovely one, but it is in the
very center of life at the Ranch, and is also in the shade
of three trees — a place which Polar Bear loved.

In any case, to me fell the job of writing the inscription
for the plaque. I did it as follows:

Beneath This Stone
Lie The Mortal Remains of
The Cat Who Came For Christmas
Beloved Polar Bear
1977–1992
'Til We Meet Again

I chose the line " 'Till We Meet Again" from the hymn
"May the Good Lord Bless and Keep You." In using that
line, it brought up the second large question — do animals
go to heaven? I do believe that we and our animals will
meet again. If we do not, and where we go is supposed
to be heaven, it will not be heaven to me and it will not
be where I wish to go.

I remember once having an argument with a Catholic
priest. Our argument had started on the subject of cruelty
to animals in general, but it soon went on into the matter
of whether or not animals went to heaven. I said that I
had been told that somewhere in the Bible, it said that
Jesus would someday come down from heaven again,
leading an army on white horses. If animals did not go

to heaven, I asked the good Father, then where did the horses come from?

Unfortunately, I had the wrong man. The good Father was one who believed in the old Catholic dogma that animals have no souls. Having heard this nonsense before, I responded to it, rather crossly and at some length. I said that the Episcopal Church to which I belonged might not be as big on souls as the Catholic Church, but if and when the good Father and I shuffled off this mortal coil, and we were going to some glorious Elysian Fields — and here I added that being Episcopalian, I might get a little better place up there than he did, but that Episcopalians were very democratic, and I would do the best I could for him — but animals were not, according to him, going anywhere, then it seemed to me all the more important that we should at least give them a little better shakes in the one life they did have.

I feel I won the argument — one of the very few I believe I have ever won with someone who was far more learned on all areas of the subject than I was. Of course I realize our argument had not settled the matter of whether or not animals went to heaven. But I had at least settled something — that, if they did not, then we owed them even more.

Certainly in just knowing Polar Bear, let alone being owned by him, I feel I owed him more than I could ever repay, let alone say. To me he was, and will always be, as I said at the beginning of this book, the best cat ever. I called him that, as I also said, in the special moments we had together, and I will always think of him as that.

I also wrote in the inscription on Polar Bear's monument

that we will meet again. I am not deeply religious, and when the subject comes up, it usually makes me nervous. And when something makes me nervous, I am inclined to make a joke about it. Years ago, for example, when I was working for the *Saturday Evening Post* and my job was choosing cartoons for the magazine, one of the first I chose was a drawing of two angels in heaven with one of them saying to the other, "Do you believe in the heretofore?"

Nonetheless, heretofore or hereafter aside, what I wrote on Polar Bear's monument I do believe — that we will meet again. And if I do not always believe it, I always try to believe it, because I also believe that if you try hard enough to believe something you will in time believe it. And one thing I know is that, when Polar Bear and I do meet again, the first thing I will say to him is that he is the best cat ever. And another thing I know is that, wherever we are, he will be the best cat there, too.

Acknowledgments

First of all, the author wishes to acknowledge the critical judgment of Marian Probst, his longtime assistant — a judgment which, hard as it is for him to bear, was amply and often demonstrated in these pages to be infuriatingly superior to his own.

Second, the author also wishes to pay tribute to the considerable contribution of his longtime editor at Little, Brown and Company, Fredrica Friedman. Although she has been singled out in the text as being two parts panther and one part Bengal tiger, it should not be forgotten that these qualities prove of particularly rare value in a book about a cat.

Third and finally, the author wishes to extend special thanks to Sean O'Gara, who somehow managed, on machines incomprehensible to the author, both to push the manuscript forward and at the same time to keep impeccable order in the office — with the exception, of course, of the office cats.

Besides this, the author is grateful for permission to quote from the following works:

"How Old Is Old?" by Ian Dunbar, D.V.M., published in April 1991 *Cat Fancy*. Reprinted by permission of the author.

The New Natural Cat: A Complete Guide for Finicky Owners by Anitra Frazier with Norma Eckroate. Copyright © 1990. Reprinted by permission of the authors.

Arthritis: What Works by Dava Sobel and Arthur C. Klein. Copyright © 1989. Reprinted by permission of St. Martin's Press, Inc.

Arthritis by Mike Samuels, M.D., and Nancy Samuels. Copyright © 1991. Reprinted by permission of Simon & Schuster, Inc.

Excerpts from the "Art and Dusty" videotape, produced by The Changes: Support for People and Pets Program at Colorado State University's Veterinary Teaching Hospital. Reprinted by permission of Carolyn Butler and Laurel Lagoni, codirectors of the program.

Courage Is a Three-Letter Word by Walter Anderson. Copyright © 1986. Reprinted by permission of Random House, Inc.